the COMPLETE *Wedding* G·U·I·D·E

D E N I S E   G R E I G

First published in the United Kingdom in 1991
by Bookmart Limited
Desford Road
Enderby
Leicester LE9 5AD

by arrangement with CollinsAngus&Robertson Publishers Pty Limited, Sydney, Australia

First published in 1991 in Australia by CollinsAngus&Robertson Publishers Pty Limited
an imprint of HarperCollins Publishers
Unit 4, Eden Park Industrial Estate,
31 Waterloo Road, North Ryde, New South Wales, 2113, Australia

ISBN 0 207 17286 2.

Typeset in Australia by Midland Typesetters
Printed in Singapore

≈ C O N T E N T S ≈

I
TRADITIONAL
≈ WEDDINGS ≈

≈ T R A D I T I O N A L ≈
W E D D I N G S

≈ THE CEREMONY ≈

As soon as the engagement is official you can start planning your wedding.

Setting the Day

Some couples announce their engagement at a party, others simply insert a notice in the newspaper.

Planning Your Wedding

A three to six months' engagement will give everyone plenty of time to enjoy wedding preparations and to ensure everything runs smoothly. It is an exhilarating time. Your celebration is an acknowledgment of the love the two of you share, and both of you must decide what style and size of wedding you want.

You must first consider the timing and date of your wedding. Spring and summer weddings are very popular and may need to be arranged months ahead. Summer Saturdays are the most popular wedding days.

Next you must consider the ceremony. For most people, the main decision about the ceremony is whether it should be religious or civil. If you are getting married in a church, visit your clergyman and find out on which days and at what hours your church is available. Make a definite booking. At this stage make inquiries about music for the ceremony: the church bells, the availability of the organist, and the minister's views on suitable music. Check if photographs or video recordings can be taken in the church.

If you decide on a civil ceremony, make a booking for the ceremony and find out the timing and duration of the ceremony and what documentation will be required to ensure the validity of the marriage.

After setting the date and booking the ceremony, make arrangements for the reception. Most reception venues need to be booked well in advance. Contact several caterers and hotels and compare the facilities, sample menus and costs. Choose the venue and style of catering you prefer and make a definite booking.

Perfect weddings depend so much on other people. Once the date has been decided, it is important to make some early arrangements to avoid disappointments.

Choose your bridesmaids, best man and ushers. Ideally there should be a partner for each bridesmaid.

If you're having your wedding dress made, get in touch with the dressmaker. Choose a dress that will suit the type of ceremony, time of year, budget and you.

Order your wedding cake.

Book your wedding photographer and videographer as soon as possible.

Order flowers for yourself, your attendants, the reception and the church.

Discuss with both sets of parents how many guests should be invited. Order invitations.

Make honeymoon reservations. If the honeymoon is overseas, obtain passports, visas etc.

Get it in Writing

Most printers, florists, photographers, musicians, caterers, reception centers and bakeries are prepared to give you a contract. This should always state the complete price, payment arrangements, site, date and time. Check clauses for overtime costs, service tips, and stipulations about last-minutes changes and cancellations.

Legalities

Before you get married, there are certain aspects of the law that you may need to consider, for example, the age at which you may marry without parental consent; whether either party has been married previously; the requirement that witnesses be present at the ceremony. Legal requirements for obtaining a marriage licence vary enormously and it is necessary to inquire locally as to the regulations regarding marriage licences.

Similarly, *where* a couple may be married will vary — in Australia, the United States and Canada, a couple may be married at a religious site of their choice, or anywhere within the civic official's jurisdiction; in the United Kingdom, all weddings must be conducted in a place of worship or in a building registered with the Superintendent Registrar of Marriages (unless granted a Special Licence by the Archbishop to conduct the wedding elsewhere).

Also, if you are planning a religious wedding you must conduct your wedding in accordance with the rites of your church.

Who Pays

The bride's family traditionally pays for almost the entire wedding and reception. These days, however, costs are often shared between the families. It is also not unusual for the bride and groom to make a contribution or even pay for the wedding themselves, especially if they are an older couple.

The following list is a guide to traditional custom and should be treated only as a starting point.

The bride's family pays for:

- *any press announcements*
- *the printing and mailing of wedding invitations*
- *flowers and decorations for the ceremony and reception*
- *photographers' fees and video recordings of the ceremony*
- *the bride's wedding clothes*
- *transport to take the wedding party to the ceremony*
- *entire cost of the reception*
- *wedding cake*
- *all wedding stationery.*

The groom pays for:

- *the bride's ring*
- *all church fees including those of the minister, choir, organist and bellringer*
- *transport to take himself and the best man to the ceremony, and for cars taking the whole bridal party from the ceremony to the reception*
- *flowers for the bride and her attendants, the corsages for his mother and the mother of the bride, and boutonnieres for himself, the best man, groomsmen and his father and the father of the bride*
- *gifts for the bridesmaids, and best man and groomsmen*
- *wedding gift for the bride*
- *his own wedding clothes*
- *the honeymoon expenses.*

The bridesmaids are responsible for paying for their own gowns and accessories, although the bride may choose to contribute.

Guest List

Consultation is the key to good family beginnings. In the interest of harmony and diplomacy, decide with both sets of parents how many people are to be invited to the wedding. Once the approximate number of guests has been agreed upon, the guest list can then be drawn up by both families with a minimum amount of anxiety. It is reasonable to assume that both the bride and groom will wish to invite similar numbers. However, this may not be the case if either of the couple comes from an area too far away for all the relatives or friends to attend the wedding, or if either is a member of a large family.

If you are to be married in a registry office, check how many people the marriage room can accommodate. You may need to restrict the number of guests invited to attend the ceremony. If there is a large discrepancy between the numbers invited to attend the ceremony and those to be present at the reception, a separate guest list will need to be drawn up.

Make a final count and order invitations and envelopes, remembering that you will need only one invitation for each married couple or family living at the same address with children under the age of eighteen. It is best, however, to order some extra invitations, since a slightly larger order will be much cheaper than having to reorder if you run out of invitations.

Invitations

By custom it is the duty of the bride's family to send out wedding invitations.

Invitation Etiquette

Telephone or word-of-mouth invitations are not considered suitable for a wedding, except in the case of a very small wedding when the invitations can be written by hand, printed or engraved invitations are the most convenient.

A good stationer will supply sample invitations showing different sizes, background color, styles of lettering

and wording format. There is a difference between engraved and printed script. Engraving is a more expensive process where the lettering stands out elegantly on the page; it is considered more traditionally 'correct,' however it takes longer than printing. It is considered most correct for the invitation to be engraved or printed in gray or black script on thick double-folded paper. It might also be in silver on a stiff white card. Nowadays there is a very large choice to suit almost every personality and invitations are subject only to style and taste.

Envelopes are always addressed by hand. Invest in a calligraphy pen for instant, improved handwriting. The only acceptable abbreviations in addressing wedding invitations are 'Dr,' 'Mr' and 'Mrs,' all else should be spelled out in full.

'Black tie' should be added at the foot of the invitation if you would like the male guests to wear dinner jackets. This will also give women guests an indication of the appropriate dress.

Wedding invitations could require up to four weeks for printing and should be ordered about eight to ten weeks before the event. A separate RSVP card should also be ordered, along with preaddressed envelopes for this card to be returned to whoever is hosting the wedding.

They should be mailed four weeks before the wedding to give the recipients enough time to respond. Be sure that all invitations are mailed simultaneously.

The Wording of Wedding Invitations

Invitations should be sent from whoever is acting as host for the wedding. A standard invitation with the bride's parents as hosts reads:

Mr and Mrs James White
request the honor of your presence

. . .

or

Mr and Mrs James White
request the pleasure of your company
at the marriage of their daughter

Alexandra
to
Mr John Murray

at St Mark's Church, Hamilton
on Saturday the fourth of June
Nineteen hundred and ninety one at
3:00 PM.
Reception following at
The Rhododendron, Roseville.

When divorced parents give the wedding together, invitations can be issued by both parents.

If the bride's mother has remarried and the invitation is issued jointly, it is worded:

Mrs Peter Richards
and Mr James White
request the pleasure of your company

. . .

14

If the bride's father has died and her mother has remarried, the bride's surname should appear on the invitation:

> *Mr and Mrs Peter Richards*
> *request the pleasure of your company*
> *at the marriage of her daughter*
> *Alexandra White*
> *. . .*

It is possible for the invitation to be sent by both sets of parents:

> *Mr and Mrs James White*
> *and*
> *Mr and Mrs Lionel Murray*
> *request the pleasure of your company*
> *at the marriage of*
> *Alexandra and John*
> *. . .*

If a close relative issued the invitation, it would read:

> *Miss Jane Stapleford*
> *requests the pleasure of your company*
> *at the marriage of her niece*
> *Alexandra White*

If the bride and groom are acting as hosts, the invitation would read:

> *Alexandra White and John Murray*
> *request the pleasure of your company*
> *at their marriage*
> *. . .*

If the guests are invited to the reception only, then the invitation may be worded:

> *Mr and Mrs James White*
> *request the pleasure of your company*
> *at the reception*
> *to follow the marriage of their*
> *daughter Alexandra*
> *to Mr John Murray*
> *at The Rhododendron, Roseville*
> *on Saturday, the fourth of June,*
> *at 4:30 PM.*

Wedding Apparel

The time of day and the choice of venue usually set the style of the wedding.

A Morning Wedding

The bride's dress may be long or short, depending on the style of the wedding. She may choose to wear a circlet of flowers or a veil either short or long. For a country wedding hats are also popular. The bridesmaids' outfits should be approximately the same length and degree of formality as the bride's dress and head gear. The groom can wear traditional morning dress at a very formal day time wedding. However, most prefer to wear navy, black or dark gray suits. For a summer wedding, the groom may wear a white or pale suit. Women guests usually choose to wear street-length dresses with optional hats or head covering for a church ceremony. Men usually wear suits.

An Afternoon Wedding

The bride's and bridesmaids' choice of dress can be the same as for a morning wedding. For a formal wedding the bride may choose a floor-length gown with a long veil. The groom and ushers may choose to wear traditional morning dress at a very formal wedding or dark suits. If the reception is to continue after dark, they may wear tuxedos. However, in Britain, where most weddings take place in the morning, at lunch time, or at the latest, at 3PM a tuxedo is rarely seen at a church wedding. Female guests wear street-length outfits, or cocktail wear if the reception is to continue into the evening.

An Evening Wedding

After 5:30PM the bride will probably wear a traditional long white gown and veil. The bridesmaids usually wear long dresses in a more formal style. The men may wear tuxedos with black bowties, or a white or ivory dinner jacket with formal black trousers. Female guests may wear cocktail dresses or long or short evening dresses.

Bridesmaids

The bride has the privilege of choosing the bridesmaids' dresses. They should complement the bride's wedding outfit, but not distract the eye from the bride. If a bride wears a period style, say, from the twenties or the Victorian era, then the bridesmaids' dresses could conform to that style. The dresses should be made in the same style and fabric, but not necessarily in the same color. Try to find a style which will suit each bridesmaid and can be worn on another occasion. Accessories such as sashes, gloves, shoes, bouquets or flowers in the hair could be in harmonious shades to add a touch of individuality.

Matron of Honor

Sometimes a bride asks a married sister or friend to act as her matron of honor. If she is to be the only attendant, then her outfit will be made to the style of the event. If however there are also bridesmaids in attendance, traditionally the matron of honor does not wear the same outfit as the unmarried bridesmaids.

Young Attendants

Very young bridesmaids do not need to wear the same dresses as the other bridesmaids and their dresses can be as enchanting or as pretty as you and they wish. They look beautiful in white and cream Edwardian dresses, pantaloons peeping beneath a skirt, pretty pinafores and blouses and velvet dresses. Make sure a long dress is cut just above the ankle to avoid tripping. White or pastel ballet pumps go with just about everything. Anything worn on the head should be very comfortable.

Pages look wonderful in military dress, sailor suits, kilts or black velvet suits with white shirts.

The Men in the Wedding Party

If the bridegroom wears morning dress, the other men in the bridal party, including both fathers, are expected to follow suit. The morning suits may be rented. At a slightly less formal wedding the men usually choose to wear suits, which should be a dark color — either black, navy or dark gray. Except when a groom chooses to wear a white suit, the best man is always dressed in the same way as the groom. If the wedding is after 5:30 PM, the groom may wear a tuxedo with a bowtie.

The Women in the Wedding Party

Since the mother, or close female relative, of the bride and of the groom will be on display as much as the members of the wedding party, it is

best that they compare notes about outfits beforehand. They are likely to be photographed together in family group portraits and will look best in dresses of complementary colors. It is most important that they reflect the same degree of formality.

Going-Away Clothes

It is a memorable event, so dress up. The bride's going-away clothes will depend very much on the form of holiday the honeymoon will take. Select an outfit that will allow you to make a stylish exit, but will also provide good service at your destination.

Attendants and Their Roles

The groom always has a best man, whether or not the bride has an attendant.

The Best Man

The best man is chosen by the bridegroom from among his relatives

organizer and a responsible person. The more dependable the best man is, the more smoothly the arrangements will run. He will act as chief liaison officer with the bride's mother. He will need to have an excellent memory and a good sense of humor and to be reassuring to the bride, groom and guests. The best man has to be a good mixer and capable of making a good speech.

His responsibilities are as follows:

To keep himself informed about the wedding arrangements, times, dates and names of all members of the wedding party.

Liaise with the bride's family regarding transport, boutonnieres and service sheets for the church.

Help the groom to choose his wardrobe, and ensure that his own and the groom's suits, if rented, have been collected.

or friends. Traditionally he is unmarried, but often a groom prefers to ask a married friend to act as his supporter. His duties are demanding and the groom would be well advised to choose someone who is a good

Ensure that all legal and travel documents are in order for the honeymoon and give them to the bride and groom at the reception.

Check on parking facilities at both the ceremony site and the reception.

Arrange a night out for the groom and his male friends before the wedding day — preferably not on the eve of the wedding.

Check that the ushers know what to do.

Collect the boutonnieres, for the bridegroom, himself and the ushers.

Ensure that the groom's traveling clothes have been sent to the reception.

Arrange for a car to take him and the groom to the church and ensure they are on time.

Make sure that all the church fees are paid before or after the ceremony, but not in front of the guests.

Safeguard the wedding ring until the groom requires it during the ceremony.

Accompany the chief bridesmaid to the vestry and sign the registry as a witness to the marriage.

Organize the cars leaving the church in the right order: the bride and groom first, followed by the parents of the bride and groom.

Make sure that all guests have transportation to the reception.

Give the speech in response to the bridegroom's toast to the bridesmaids.

Read out the messages of congratulations that have been received.

Put the couple's luggage in the honeymoon car.

Drive the couple to the airport or railway station if necessary.

Collect the groom's wedding suit after the reception and either return it to the rental company or look after it until the groom returns.

The Maid of Honor

Traditionally the chief bridesmaid is the bride's eldest unmarried sister or a very close friend. If married, the chief bridesmaid is known as the matron of honor and will dress slightly different from the other attendants.

The chief bridesmaid or matron of honor is not as concerned as the best man with making arrangements, but is expected to help the bride as much as possible. Some of her responsibilities are as follows:

Attend all the prewedding parties; she may wish to give one herself.

Help the bride to dress for her wedding.

Ensure that the other bridesmaids are properly dressed and ready on time.

Wait at the church entrance for the bride and organize any child attendants.

Arrange the bride's veil and train before the procession down the aisle.

Take charge of the bride's bouquet and gloves during the service.

Help draw the bride's veil clear of her face.

Return the bride's bouquet to her to carry in the procession leaving the ceremony.

Stand in the receiving line with the bride and groom at the reception.

Be available during the reception to give the bride any help required, including attending to presents or keeping a watchful eye on small attendants.

Help the bride change into her going-away clothes.

Take charge of the bride's wedding clothes.

Bridesmaids

The number of bridesmaids the bride chooses depends on the size and style of the wedding. Their main duties are to help the bride in any way they can in the weeks before the wedding and on the wedding day.

Some of the bridesmaids' responsibilities are as follows:

Help display the gifts.

Take part in the wedding procession, following the chief bridesmaid in pairs or single file if numbers are uneven.

If she desires, stand with the bride in the receiving line at the reception.

Circulate among the guests.

Give the bride any help and support she may need during the period leading up to the wedding.

Attend any prewedding parties or arrange one themselves.

Assemble at the bride's home prior to the ceremony to receive their bouquets.

Assist in getting the bride ready for the ceremony.

Groomsmen or Male Attendants

Groomsmen or male attendants are usually close friends or relatives of the bride or groom. There should be enough groomsmen to partner each bridesmaid. They attend the bachelor party if there is one. Groomsmen are responsible for their own clothes which are similiar to those worn by the groom. At the reception they are seated at the bridal table, but do not stand in the receiving line. They are expected to circulate among the guests. Groomsmen are not common in the United Kingdom.

Ushers

At a formal church wedding of fifty or more guests it is helpful to have ushers to meet guests as they arrive and escort them to their seats. The groom usually chooses the ushers from among his or his bride's brothers and friends. It is best if the ushers chosen know most of the guests. There should be at least one usher for every fifty guests.

Their responsibilities are as follows:

Hand out service sheets to guests and show them to their places at the ceremony. Relatives and friends of the bride sit on the seats on the left and those of the groom on the right.

Escort the bride's mother to the aisle corner seat in the front left row.

The chief usher should tell the groom that the bride has arrived, and inform the organist that it is time to begin the processional music.

After the ceremony, ushers should assist the best man in ensuring that all the guests have transportation from the ceremony to the reception.

Show the guests to their place at the reception.

Flower Girls and Pages

Young attendants can lend a special charm to a formal wedding. They are usually brothers or sisters of the couple or other close relatives. The flower girl walks at the head of the procession down the aisle.

Pages or trainbearers usually walk in pairs following the bride down the aisle, and holding her train. In some services, a page carrying the ring on a velvet cushion walks with the flower girl in front of the bride.

Timing it Right at the Church

Before the day, you will almost certainly have the opportunity to rehearse the ceremony. The ushers who show guests to their places should be the first to arrive, and should arrive at least a half an hour before the ceremony. They should hand out service sheets or hymn books to the guests on arrival at the ceremony and show them to their seats.

Let Us Be Seated

In church it is usual for the bride's family and guests to occupy pews on the left hand side of the church and for the groom's family and guests to sit on the right. The bride's eldest brother or the chief usher should escort the bride's mother to the left front pew. The groom's parents are seated in the right front pew.

The bridegroom and best man should arrive at the church twenty minutes before the ceremony. They wait until a few minutes before the bride is due and then take up position standing at the right of the center aisle in front of the congregation.

The bridesmaids and pages wait at the entrance to the church for the arrival of the bride. The bride and her father are the last to arrive. Tradition tells us that it is lucky for the bride to arrive late, but in case of unforeseen delays

she should aim to be at the church exactly on time. The bridesmaids attend to her dress and train. Her veil should be over her face as she enters the church. The organist then begins to play the processional music and the guests rise.

Order of the Bridal Procession

If there is a flower girl, she leads the procession. Otherwise the chief bridesmaid or matron of honor leads the way, followed by the other bridesmaids in pairs or single file, and finally the bride and her father. If the service is fully choral, the choir leads the procession followed by the minister, the bride on her father's arm and the attendants.

When they reach the end of the aisle, the bride's father should lead her to the bridegroom's left. He then stands to her left. Once they are in position, the maid or matron of honor steps forward to take the bride's bouquet, and gloves if she is wearing them. This is a good time to set the bride's veil back over her head, clear of her face. However, it may be a good idea to first check with the minister before the ceremony if there is any particular time when he prefers the veil to be pulled back. For the duration of the ceremony, the bride wears her engagement ring on the third finger of her right hand, returning it to her left hand afterward.

The bridesmaids stand slightly to the left behind the bride. The best man stands at the right of the groom but a little behind him, and behind the groom stand the groomsmen or male attendants.

Order of Service

The order of the service varies according to the denomination, the views of the minister and the wishes of the couple. Some ministers prefer to perform the marriage ceremony before any hymns are sung, but you may want a hymn to be sung before the ceremony begins.

The vows are then taken (with or without the promise to 'obey'). You can choose to read the vows instead of repeating them after the minister.

The minister begins the chosen service by stating the reason for the gathering and the significance of marriage, and then asks if there is any reason why the couple may not lawfully marry. If there is no legal objection to the union, he proceeds with the service.

When the minister asks, 'Who giveth this woman to be married to this man?' the bride's father steps forward, takes her right hand and gives it to the minister, who then passes it into the hand of the bridegroom. The bride's father then takes his place in the front pew.

The best man gives the ring to the minister, and the bridegroom places it on the third finger of the bride's left hand. Often the bride also gives the groom a ring. The bridegroom and bride then make their vows to each other.

The Signing of the Register

As soon as the official ceremony is over, the minister takes the newly-married couple, followed by both sets of parents, the best man and

attendants to the vestry. In the vestry
the bride signs the register in her
maiden name, followed by her
husband, the minister and two

witnesses. During the signing of the
register the choir or a soloist may sing
or the organist may play a piece of
music.

Leaving the Church

When the formalities are completed,
the bridal procession leaves the church
in the following order: the bride and
bridegroom, small attendants, chief
bridesmaid or matron of honor and
best man, bridesmaids and groomsmen
or male attendants, bride's mother and
groom's father, groom's mother and
bride's father.

If there is to be a guard of honor, this
should be stationed between the
church door and the bridal car. In the
United States a guard of honor would
only be used at a military wedding.

Usually photographs are taken outside
the church. Although this important
session of photographs should not be
rushed, you should not take too long,
especially if you have a set time at the
reception rooms.

Finishing Touches

Perfect weddings begin with carefully laid plans, but it is the details that make your day very special.

Flowers

Whether your ceremony is a small family gathering or a stylish formal wedding, flowers add a beautiful and important dimension to the day. No matter what season you get married, a wide selection of beautiful flowers can fill your bouquets and decorate both the ceremony and reception areas.

Always try to select flowers that are in season during your wedding month. They will be less costly, have larger blooms and stronger stems and there will be a greater supply on the market to ensure availability. From a floral point of view, late spring to early summer is the best time to get married.

While the bride's mother or friends may sometimes be able to provide the ceremony and reception's floral arrangements, most brides prefer to have their bouquets and boutonnieres made professionally. It is advisable to consult your florist several weeks before the wedding. The florist will be able to advise what will be available and order your flower choice in advance.

When deciding your floral requirements, the main consideration will be the general color scheme and style you want to follow. Floral decorations should harmonize with the clothes of members of the wedding party and with the flowers carried by the bride and her attendants. Don't forget you will need to get the minister's permission to decorate the church.

Remember that flowers are more expensive if you want something that is out of season. To match your flowers to your wedding colors take swatches of fabric to your florist. A sketch of your gown and your bridesmaids' dresses will help in designing the style and shape of bouquets. Bridesmaids' flowers are chosen with an eye to the total bridal color scheme.

Music

Music will be an integral part of the church ceremony and you should not leave organizing it to the last minute. It will set the mood for the service — from the joyous background music played while the guests assemble to the pageantry of the bridal procession. You will need to select hymns for the service, music for the signing of the register and music for leaving the church.

You should always check your musical selection with the minister at the church. The organist will be able to help you choose selections for the church ceremony. If you are having a choir or soloist sing at your wedding, choose the music with the help of the choirmaster.

Wedding Bells

If the church possesses bells they are sometimes pealed for twenty minutes immediately prior to the ceremony and for up to half an hour afterward.

The Photographer

Your wedding photographs should bring back memories of a wonderful and happy day. To ensure that you get a high quality and complete pictorial record of your wedding, you will almost certainly want to engage a professional photographer. When choosing your photographer, look at samples of previous work. It is important to choose a photographer with whom you can feel at ease and who will capture the essence and

style of your wedding. You will need a number of formally posed photographs as well as photos which show the romance, fun and glamor of your wedding.

An experienced photographer will know how to cover a wedding, but must be told about special situations. Prepare a timetable of events or a list of situations you would like photographed. Decide whether you require the photographer's services for

the entire occasion: from early arrival at your home, to the ceremony, the reception and the departure. The photographer should be able to quote you an attendance fee. If a videographer is hired as well, these two must work out a plan together ahead of time. Remember that you will need to check with the minister about what photography is allowed in the church.

Many brides welcome the trend to take portraits at home before the ceremony. Although the couple cannot be together before the ceremony, it is still an opportune time to photograph the bride, her parents and the bridesmaids.

Wedding Rings

The wedding ring is a token of a lifelong commitment between the bridegroom and the bride. The moment it is placed on the bride's finger is often the most significant part of the ceremony.

The wedding ring is a plain or occasionally engraved band in white or yellow gold or platinum. This is the groom's gift to the bride, though today many couples like the idea of exchanging matching rings in the ceremony. It is placed on the third finger of the bride's left hand because it was once believed that this finger was connected directly to the heart by a vein.

Prior to the wedding ceremony the bride should switch her engagement ring to her right hand until after the ceremony is over, when she places it on the same finger as the wedding ring.

At a traditional reception, guests are introduced along a receiving line. This allows each guest to talk to their hosts and to congratulate the bride and groom.

The Receiving Line

To prevent long lines and delays everyone should make their greetings brief and save longer conversations until after all the guests have been received.

At a very formal reception an usher may ask the name of each guest and announce it to the bride's parents, who in turn will introduce the guest to whoever is standing next to them and so on down the line.

The receiving line consists of the bride's mother and father, the groom's mother and father, the bride and groom, the chief bridesmaid and the matron of honor, and the bridesmaids.

If a less formal receiving line is required, then the bride's mother stands at the entrance to the reception with the bride and groom, with the groom's parents next in line. If you wish to dispense with the custom altogether, then the guests can be received by the bride and groom only. At a large wedding this saves a great deal of time.

The best man and ushers never stand in the receiving line. Instead they should circulate, be helpful and introduce guests to each other. Child attendants seldom have to stand in line.

Both the women and the men in the receiving line should shake hands with the guests. If you are wearing gloves, you may leave them on, but it seems friendlier to remove them. A small table should be conveniently placed to hold the bouquets.

The receiving line should not break up until every guest has been greeted.

It is customary for the waiters to serve drinks while the guests are being received. As soon as all the guests have passed into the reception hall, the bridal party circulates among the guests. Shortly afterward they take their seats at the main table if a sit-down meal is to be served. At the same time the chief usher directs guests to their tables according to the seating plan.

Seating Plan

At a large wedding it is usual to have a seating plan and place cards.

The Bridal Table

The bride and groom sit in the places of honor. The placing should be designed to accommodate all the members of the wedding party as well as both sets of parents. Sometimes changes may have to be made in order to accommodate divorced parents and their partners.

The official table for the bridal party faces the guests, with the bride and groom in the central positions. The bride always sits on the groom's left. The bride's mother sits on the groom's right and the bride's father on the bride's left. The groom's father sits next to the bride's mother and the groom's mother next to the bride's father. The best man is on the left of the groom's mother and the chief bridesmaid or matron of honor on the right of the groom's father. Alternatively, the best man and maid of honor can be seated beside the bride and groom, with the parents further out from the centre. The other attendants sit on either side. As far as possible, men and women should alternate.

At many receptions there is a separate table near the bridal table for the couple's parents. This can be especially useful when accommodating divorced parents and new partners. In the seating arrangements it is best to separate divorced parents and to keep the present partners together. The grandparents and godparents should sit at the parents' table if there is room. If the officiating clergyman and his wife attend the reception, they usually sit with the parents, but may sit with the wedding party.

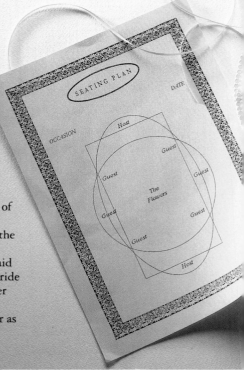

SEATING PLAN

DATE

OCCASION

Host

Guest

Guest

Guest

Guest

The Flowers

Guest

Guest

Guest

Host

Seating the Wedding Guests

Depending on the space available, the caterer will advise you on a workable seating plan to suit the number of guests. If there are more than fifty guests, it is advisable to have a seating plan and place cards. The table plan should be placed in a convenient position so that guests can easily find their table number. If there are place cards on the table, they will find their seats without difficulty.

As a wedding reception is an ideal opportunity for the two families and friends to get to know each other better, try to mix the seating at the tables. Try to place people together who you feel will like each other, and give some thought to such problems as family feuds. The closer a guest is to the bridal table, the more honored he or she will be.

At a religious wedding, after everybody has found his or her place, the best man or master of ceremonies asks for silence for grace to be said. If you have a clergyman present, it is customary to ask him to say grace.

Master of Ceremonies

Often the best man or an old family friend fulfills the role of master of ceremonies. He will invite guests to be seated and announce the cutting of the cake, the toasts and speeches and the bridal waltz.

The Cutting of the Cake

This is one of the highlights of the reception. The cake-cutting ceremony takes place at the end of the meal after the speeches, although some brides prefer to cut the cake immediately before the toasts and speeches to allow sufficient time for it to be sliced and served with the coffee or as the dessert. The bride puts her right hand on top of the handle of the knife and the groom puts his right hand on top of hers. Together they carefully cut the first slice. This is a good time for the champagne to be handed around.

Toasts and Speeches

Speeches are not essential at weddings, but most families would not feel the celebrations complete unless the health and happiness of the newlyweds had been drunk immediately following the cutting of the wedding cake.

Toasts should be kept to a minimum and speeches should be brief, entertaining and witty. Glasses should be replenished for the toasts.

The traditional formal order of toasts and speeches is as follows:

The toast to the bride and groom is proposed by a close friend or relative of the bride's family. This toast is to wish the couple health, happiness and prosperity.

The couple remain seated and do not drink the toast.

The groom responds to this toast and thanks everyone on behalf of his wife

The best man replies for the bridesmaids. He also reads the messages of congratulations and good wishes that have arrived for the newlyweds.

and himself. He thanks the bride's parents for their daughter's hand in marriage and for the reception. He also thanks the guests for their good wishes, for attending the wedding and for their gifts. He thanks the best man for his support and finishes by proposing a toast to the bridemaids.

A number of other toasts are possible. The best man, master of ceremonies or a family friend may toast the parents of the bride and groom. The bride's father and the father of the groom may wish to respond after the appropriate toast.

Dancing and Music

While it is not essential to have music at the reception, it will provide a pleasant background and is the easiest way to entertain. It will also provide the ideal opportunity for all to join in the celebration through dancing. At the reception you might choose a pianist, a guitarist, a quartet, a group or a disc jockey to provide the music.

If there is to be dancing, select music that will appeal to a wide range of ages and musical tastes.

Music should be playing when the first guests arrive at the reception. Background music is played until the receiving line is disbanded, and dinner music or light jazz is often played during the meal. Dancing music may be played before the meal and continue between courses or begin after the meal.

When hiring musicians, find out how many breaks they will take and for how long. If you want music throughout the reception, hire a second musician, or arrange for tapes to be played on a sound system.

The First Dance

It is important that the bride and groom begin the dancing. The bride's parents then join them on the floor.

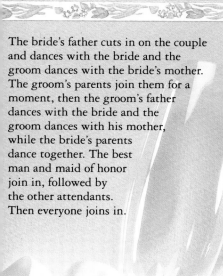

The bride's father cuts in on the couple
and dances with the bride and the
groom dances with the bride's mother.
The groom's parents join them for a
moment, then the groom's father
dances with the bride and the
groom dances with his mother,
while the bride's parents
dance together. The best
man and maid of honor
join in, followed by
the other attendants.
Then everyone joins in.

Leaving the Reception

After a few hours the couple slips away
to change from the wedding attire into
going-away clothes. Traditionally
guests should not leave the reception
before the bride, so it is considerate for
the bride and groom not to stay at the
reception all night or spend too long
changing.

bouquet over her shoulder. This can be done before the bride changes or just before the couple leaves on their honeymoon.

The custom of throwing the garter originated in sixteenth-century France, when pieces of bridal attire were considered lucky. The tossing of the garter takes place just after the bride tosses the bouquet. The groom removes the garter from the bride's leg and throws it over his shoulder to a crowd of single men. The man who catches it is said to be destined to be the next to wed. At many weddings nowadays, he places the garter on the leg of the woman who caught the bridal bouquet.

After changing, the couple returns to the guests for a few minutes before going on their honeymoon.

Traditionally, the bride tosses her bouquet to the young women gathered. The one who catches the bouquet is supposed to be the next to marry. To show no favoritism, the bride turns her back and tosses the

≈ WEDDING PRESENTS AND ≈
THANK-YOU NOTES

Soon after the wedding invitations have been sent out, presents will begin to arrive for the engaged couple.

Wedding Presents

Wedding presents should always be addressed to the bride at her home. Often friends and relatives telephone the bride's mother to find out what the couple would like as a wedding present. It is quite acceptable for you to compile a fairly extensive gift list in order to give guests guidance and to save them from duplicating presents. The list should include items at all price levels and mention should be made of your particular choice of product, style or color. Many large stores have a gift registry and a consultant who will help you compile a list. Guests can see the list at the store, and the consultant will ensure there are no duplications.

Occasionally the wedding presents are displayed at the reception, but more often the presents are exhibited at the bride's home. Sometimes a display may be arranged at the couple's new home when they return from their honeymoon. Each present should be displayed with its card. In the case of a sum of money, only the envelope is displayed stating the name of the donor. The amount of the check should not be divulged.

It is also a common practice for the bridegroom to present each of the bridesmaids with a small gift either before the wedding or during the reception. The groom is also responsible for gifts to the best man, groomsmen or male attendants and pages.

Thank-You Notes

A thoughtful, prompt note of thanks should be written for each wedding gift received.

If possible, thank-you notes should be sent before you set off on your honeymoon. Gifts that arrive near or after the wedding day should be acknowledged within a month after your honeymoon. Writing thank-yous as soon as you receive the gifts makes it easier for the wording to be enthusiastic and spontaneous. It will also help keep the task manageable.

Traditionally the writing of such notes has been the duty of the bride. To make the job easier and more fun, ask your groom to help, especially with the notes to his relatives and friends. Thank-you notes should always be hand written and worded from both partners. However, only the writer should sign each note. The bride should use her maiden name for notes written before the wedding.

Be Methodical

A systematic way of keeping check on gifts and thank-yous is to keep a notebook, file or computer list of the guest list with the address, date, gift

received, detailed description of the gift and date the thank-you note was sent. This will save a lot of time and stress if you are having a large wedding.
    Including details of the gift on your list enables you to make easy reference to the gift itself — an important part of a thoughtful thank-you note.

Letters of thanks should not be typewritten or printed. If the couple receives a very large number of gifts, a printed card may be sent,

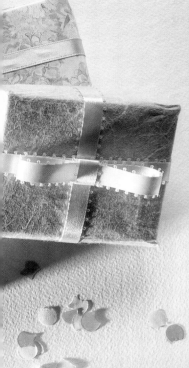

acknowledging that the gift arrived safely. This should be followed as soon as possible by the bride's or groom's hand-written note of appreciation.

The traditional thank-you note is written in blue or black ink on white or ivory stationery, although any conservative color is suitable. Some couples choose to have the paper monogrammed with their name or initials. Personalized notepaper should be ordered well before the wedding— preferably when ordering invitations — so that notes can be sent out soon after you return from your honeymoon.

Each note should say something about the gift and how you plan to use it. Try to include at least one other personal message, such as an invitation to visit.

If a gift is received that will be exchanged, express your appreciation for the gesture of kindness. Whether or not you inform the donor of your intention is entirely up to you.

Those who have sent messages of congratulations should also be acknowledged and thanked.

II
≈ WEDDING FLOWERS ≈

≈ WEDDING FLOWERS ≈

≈ SELECTING FLOWERS ≈

A bride's choice of flowers may be traditional or informal, lavish or simple, romantic or elegant. The bride's choice of flowers, like the choice of dress design and fabrics, will help evoke a mood. Whatever her choice, flowers should be in harmony with her personality, her wedding dress and her style of wedding.

Fragrant Flowers

When one thinks of fragrant wedding flowers, pure white orange blossoms immediately spring to mind. For centuries Eastern and Saracen brides wore or carried orange blossoms. The tradition began in Europe at the time of the Crusaders and fortunately has stayed with us.

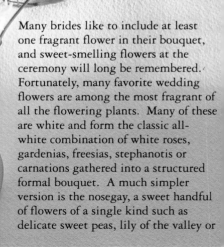

Many brides like to include at least one fragrant flower in their bouquet, and sweet-smelling flowers at the ceremony will long be remembered. Fortunately, many favorite wedding flowers are among the most fragrant of all the flowering plants. Many of these are white and form the classic all-white combination of white roses, gardenias, freesias, stephanotis or carnations gathered into a structured formal bouquet. A much simpler version is the nosegay, a sweet handful of flowers of a single kind such as delicate sweet peas, lily of the valley or a tiny bunch of snowdrops like those carried by Queen Victoria on her wedding day.

Large bowls of freesias, tuberoses, stock and trailing jasmine distributed around the church will provide a memorable fragrance at the ceremony. Tiny posies of daphne or gardenias can be attached to the end of the rows of seats to greet wedding guests as they take their places. If the wedding is to be held in a large musky church, consider placing bunches of the more pleasant-smelling scented geraniums strategically around the church so they may be brushed against and their scent released. The peppermint scented *Pelargonium tomentosum*, for example, has a particularly refreshing fragrance as well as attractively shaped leaves.

At the reception large arrangements of boughs of apple blossoms will provide charm, romance and a light fragrance. Carnations have a soft scent and are perfect for table decorations, whereas

freesias and gardenias may be too overpowering. A small herbal arrangement composed of both leaf and blossom may be just the right table centerpiece for your style of wedding.

Color Themes

Color is used more and more often in bridal bouquets, for it can offset a dress or be used to unify the whole bridal party, and many brides like to coordinate the color theme of the bridal party to the flowers used at the ceremony and reception. If the bride is wearing white and the bridesmaids deep pink, for example, the bride's bouquet might consist of a mixture of white and deep pink roses. The bridesmaids could carry miniature pink and white rose buds and the men wear deep pink rose boutonnieres. Deep pink hydrangeas, dahlias and chrysanthemums highlighted with lots of white flowers could be used at the ceremony and reception.

Therefore when choosing your flowers, it is important that you plan your color scheme very carefully. If you have a very set idea about what color flowers you want to carry on your wedding day — red roses, for instance, or blue cornflowers — choose your flowers first before deciding on the color of your bridesmaids' dresses.

The amount of color used depends on the color theme the bride wants to carry out, but generally two or three colors, including white, work well together.

Shades of White

Traditionally white flowers connote the bride's purity. Flower fashions come and go, but an all-white bouquet is still a favorite. White roses, orchids, gardenias, lilac, camellias, stephanotis, tulips and lily of the valley are among the most popular choices for a very formal wedding. The bouquet may be made of a single variety of flowers, or it may be a combination of several.

If you plan to wear a pure white fabric, match it with pure white flowers such as orchids, hyacinths and stephanotis. If however your fabric will be off-white, you might wish to consider a bouquet using shades of white and silver, cream and gray. Sweet peas, stock, ranunculus, foxgloves and old-fashioned roses, the most romantic flowers of all, have lovely off-white hues. These flowers look particularly beautiful with antique lace and off-white satin.

All-white arrangements at the ceremony and reception might include some bold flowers such as giant chrysanthemums, lilies, dahlias, gladiolus, agapanthus and branches of azaleas, softened by baby's breath, Queen Anne's lace, trailing jasmine and ivy.

Pink Flowers

Pink flowers are a popular choice with brides and always look good combined with white or cream. Different shades of pink work well together and look pretty with a touch of lilac. Flowers in shades of pink are ideal for a large wedding as they are available at different times of the year, large quantities are ensured and the price will therefore not be prohibitive. Roses, carnations, sweet peas, peonies, freesias, chrysanthemums, camellias, tulips, stock and dahlias all make beautiful bouquets. Dainty nerines come in many beautiful shades of pink, and in stripes, and should not be overlooked as a bouquet flower in autumn. Armfuls of azaleas, rhododendrons, hydrangeas, larkspurs, hollyhocks and fruit blossoms can be gleaned from gardens to decorate the ceremony and reception.

Blue, Mauve and Purple Flowers

Under some lighting conditions
flowers in shades of blue do not always
come true to color in photographs. If
this does not worry you and blue
flowers are your favorites, make a
feature of them at the ceremony and
reception. Hydrangeas, delphiniums,
agapanthus and lupines combined
with white and a splash of yellow
make a spectacular large arrangement.
Blue combined with a bright clear
orange can also look very effective.
Cornflowers, hyacinths, sweet peas,
scabious, love-in-a-mist and forget-
me-nots make charming small
bouquets and can be repeated in
miniature as table decorations at the
reception. Blue-green or gray foliage
can be used to balance blue flowers in
an arrangement.

Yellow Flowers

The combination of yellow and white flowers is a popular color theme for weddings. Yellow flowers enliven bouquets and arrangements and their color reproduces beautifully in photographs.

Yellow flowers need to be chosen carefully to tone in with bridesmaids' dresses. Some yellow roses, for example, lean toward a cream color, and if the bridesmaids are to wear lemon this would not work. Carnations, chrysanthemums, daffodils, dahlias, freesias, gerberas, iris, orchids, tulips and roses all come in different shades of yellow, and you will need to specify exactly what tone you require.

Red and Orange Flowers

Many brides are breaking with tradition and choosing strongly colored, vibrant flowers to highlight their gowns. Unstructured bouquets look particularly good with red or orange blooms. A spray of coral-colored orchids or unusual flowers such as vallota and the exotic waxy anthurium add a touch of brilliant elegance to a bridal bouquet and are perfect with a modern gown.

Red roses symbolize love, and many brides carry them on their wedding day. Long-stemmed red roses carried by a tall elegant bride look sensational at a formal daytime wedding. If you are getting married late in the afternoon or in the evening, choose red roses with a hint of coral or deep pink roses, as very dark red roses do not photograph well under lower light and can look very harsh against wedding finery.

Nasturtiums, calendulas and gerberas have a timeless quality and make cheerful table decorations for a country wedding. Large sprays of red berries used with variegated foliage make beautiful ceremony and reception arrangements for an autumn wedding.

Green Flowers

An all-green flower theme can provide an enchanting touch, especially if the bride and her attendants are wearing white. Choose one variety of green flower, or mix different varieties of green flowers with a little foliage. Arum lilies, bells of Ireland, hydrangea, lady's mantle, lime blossoms, nicotiana, sea holly and zinnia all produce green flowers at different times of the year and will produce a different mood for each season.

Keeping Flowers Fresh

Most florists make up the bouquets, headpieces and corsages the day before or on the day of the wedding. Should it be a hot day, the florist will give instructions on the best way of keeping them fresh. Bouquets with exposed stems can simply be placed in a vase of water. If flowers are wired with wrapped stems, they are usually enclosed in clear cellophane that has been gently misted inside. If flowers are delivered in a box, leave them there until you are ready. They should be kept in the coolest room in the house, out of bright sunlight.

Usually the floral arrangements at the ceremony and reception are prepared the day before the wedding. Ensure that someone checks that they are fresh on the day of the wedding. Any flowers that have wilted should be removed, the vases should be topped up with water if necessary, and the flowers lightly sprayed with water.

The Language of Flowers

In literature many references are made to flowers and their specific meanings. For those with a romantic imagination, the following list will help you choose flowers and foliage with special symbolism for your bouquet:

Apple Blossom *Preference*

Azalea *Temperance*

Buttercup
Memories of childhood

Camellia, white *Perfected loveliness*

Carnation *Bonds of affection; pure love*

Chrysanthemum, white *Truth*

Cornflower *Hope*

Daffodil *Regard*

Dahlia *Instability*

Daisy *Innocence*

Fern *Fascination*

Forget-me-not
True love

Gardenia
Secret untold love

Geranium, ivy
Bridal favor

Geranium, oak-leaved
True friendship

Geranium, rose-scented *Preference*

Honeysuckle *Generosity*

Hyacinth *Constancy*

Hydrangea *Boasting*

Iris *Message*

Jasmine *Amiability*

Jonquil
*I desire a return
of affection*

Larkspur *Fickleness*

Lavender *Distrust*

Lilac *First love*

Lily, white
Purity

Lily of the Valley
Return of happiness

Mimosa
Sensitivity

Mint *Virtue*

Myrtle *Love*

Nasturtium
Patriotism

Orange Blossom
Chastity

Pansy *Love; courtship*

Rose *Love*

Rosemary *Remembrance*

Sage *Riches; health*

Snowdrop *Hope*

Stock *Beauty*

Sweet Pea *Pleasure*

Tulip *Fame*

Tulip, red
Declaration of love

Violet *Faithfulness*

Zinnia
Thoughts of absent friends

≈ THE FLORIST ≈

Be sure to consult an experienced florist in order to have good advice on seasonal considerations, style and cost.

Working with a Florist

The bride's mother is responsible for decorating the sites of the ceremony and the reception. A creative mother of the bride, or members of the family or friends, may be very capable of doing the church and reception arrangements themselves. Many brides, however, prefer their bouquets, corsages, headpieces and special arrangements to be prepared by a professional florist. Even an unstructured armful of flowers tied together with ribbon will require the special artistry of the florist to prevent the bruising of flowers and to keep the bouquet fresh and beautiful throughout the ceremony and reception.

If possible it is best to consult a florist at least two months before the wedding. The florist will work out your floral requirements and be able to advise what colors will be available in the varieties you choose during your wedding season. You will be able to choose the bouquet styles from photographs of a selection of designs. This will give you an idea of the range of shapes, sizes and compositions available. The florist can also advise on the suitability of certain flowers for the church and reception.

Flowers prepared by a professional can be very expensive, so before you make a firm booking, shop around. Flowers are more expensive if you want something that is out of season and has to be imported. Both locally grown flowers and flowers in season are generally less costly.

To match your flowers to your wedding colors, take along fabric samples to your florist. A sketch of your dress and those of the bridesmaids can be helpful in choosing designs for the bouquets.

Ask for a quote in writing for each item and inquire about delivery arrangements.

Traditionally, the bridegroom pays for the flowers carried or worn by the bride and bridesmaids, the corsages for the mother of the bride and of the groom and the boutonnieres for the male members of the bridal party, including the father of the bride and of the groom.

Although it is customary for the groom to pay for the bouquets and boutonnieres, he should allow the bride to choose her own wedding flowers and, at the same time, order the church and reception flowers from the same florist.

Florist's Calendar

No matter what season you get married, there is a wide selection of beautiful flowers available that will fill your bouquets and decorate the ceremony and reception areas.

There are far too many different species of flowers to list them all. The following is a very general seasonal guide to the availability of popular wedding flowers:

Spring and Summer

Agapanthus
Alstroemeria
Apple blossom
Astilbe
Camellia
Cornflower
Daffodil
Dahlia
Delphinium
Gladiolus
Honeysuckle
Hyacinth
Hydrangea
Jasmine
Jonquil
Lavender
Lilac
Lily of the Valley
Magnolia
Mock orange

Peony
Ranunculus
Snapdragon
Statice
Stephanotis
Stock
Strawflower
Sweet pea
Tuberose
Tulip
Zinnia

Autumn and Winter

Amaryllis
Bouvardia
Camellia
Christmas rose
Chrysanthemum
Cotoneaster (berries)
Cyclamen
Dahlia
Daphne
Gardenia
Holly (berries)
Hyacinth
Muscari
Nerine
Peach Blossom
Stephanotis
Tuberose
Viburnum

Popular Wedding Flowers Available Year-round

Alstroemeria
Anemone
Arum Lily
Azalea
Baby's breath
Bells of Ireland
Carnation
Cattleya orchid
Chincherinchee
Cymbidium orchid
Dendrobium orchid
Freesia
Gerbera
Gladiolus
Iris
Lilies
Marguerite daisy
Queen Anne's lace
Rose

≈ FLOWERS FOR THE BRIDE ≈

Headpieces

A headpiece finishes the bride's look by uniting dress and hair. One of the most charming and romantic ways to enhance a bridal look is to wear fresh flowers as an adornment for the head.

Flowers that are dainty but with good keeping qualities should be considered when selecting material for headpieces. Miniature roses, hyacinth florets, stephanotis, tuberose, baby's breath and tiny carnations will all remain fresh-looking.

Hair decorations may include a spray of flowers attached to a comb, a floral tiara, a half circlet worn across the top of the head or a full circlet of flowers.

A small circlet can also be worn around a bun or to tie back long hair. Select a headpiece that continues the theme from your gown and that suits you and your hairstyle.

Headpieces may be worn with or without a veil. A small circlet covered in tiny blossoms that sits high on the head will provide a lovely anchor for a wedding veil. A half circlet worn at the back of the head, will hold a trailing veil beautifully.

For short hair try a floral wreath worn on the brow. Accent a chignon with a profile comb decorated with beautiful orchids. A tiara of flowers can be worn with or without a veil and will complement any hair length.

Traditional Bridal Bouquets

While some brides have their heart set on a classic bouquet composed of elegant white flowers, others want their wedding bouquet to be an armful of unstructured country flowers. Whatever your choice of design, your bouquet should complement your wedding dress, but should not assume undue importance. Although the bride's flowers take pride of place, they should not be so large that they hide the beauty of the bridal gown.

The style of the bride's bouquet will depend on the bride's height and build. Large bouquets such as the stunning formal cascade of white roses carried by Princess Diana are best carried by tall brides. A shorter bride should choose a smaller tapering cascade of flowers of medium length. Similarly, the effect of a tiny Victorian posy would be lost on a large or tall bride, but would be a good choice for a petite bride.

The style of the gown and the texture of its fabric is also to be considered. If the dress is straight and severe, consider carrying long-stemmed roses or a strongly shaped bouquet of perhaps lilies or orchids. If it has a softly falling skirt, a smallish wispy bouquet with lots of cascading ribbons is a lovely complement. With a lace or heavily appliqued dress use a simple, elegant design with plain ribbon tails. A richly textured sheaf of lilies would be perfect for a classic satin gown. Camellias and gardenias with their sculptured shiny leaves are also beautiful against a satin or brocade dress.

The choice of forms and flowers is almost unlimited. Some traditional designs are given here, but many more may be created from the abundance of floral material available.

Cascade or Shower Bouquet

This is probably the most popular form of traditional bridal bouquet. It is a teardrop shape and is made in two sections — a bouquet section and a trailer. When joined together the bouquet looks as if it were made as one tapering piece. Its classic style makes it an appropriate accompaniment to a formal gown with a long train in any season. The bouquet may be made using a single variety of flowers such as orchids or it may consist of a combination of several, for example, roses, gardenias, carnations and stephanotis.

Crescent Bouquet

A crescent bouquet has a small central posy with two trails either side, pointed slightly downward to form a crescent shape. It can be used to echo the line or feature of a dress. Miniature roses, stephanotis, or small white orchids on their own work well with this design.

Rounded Bouquet

A plump rounded bouquet is made the same way as a posy, except that more flowers are used and layers are built up higher to form a dome. This is a popular form of bridal bouquet and, depending on the flowers chosen, may be as exquisite or as romantic as the bride wishes. A very lightly wired mass of pastel roses interspersed with lily of the valley and tied with matching trailing ribbons is a beautiful choice for a romantic wedding.

Sheaf Bouquet

The elegant, elongated shape of a sheaf is popular with tall brides. A sheaf may be made with a variety of spike flowers such as tuberose, delphiniums, lilac, gladiolus, ixia and arum lilies. When choosing flowers for a sheaf, avoid large heavy blooms, as you will have to carry the flowers for some time. It is possible to have a miniature sheaf made of lily of the valley, small rosebuds or a simple bouquet made of long-stemmed tulips tied with satin ribbon.

Trailers

There are two main types of floral trailers. The first is designed to be carried with a prayer book. The second is finished with a ribbon handle and is carried alone. Very beautiful trailers can be made using a single flower species such as a few gardenias and their handsome foliage or with a combination of two or three flowers such as carnations, nerines and stephanotis.

Posies

Posies were once mostly carried by bridesmaids, but these days more and more brides are choosing a Victorian-style posy to suit a period gown. A posy is a tight rounded arrangement of small and medium-sized flowers gathered into a handle and backed with an old-fashioned paper doily. Sometimes a posy is backed with a puff of tulle or is made from lace that has been included in the bride's or bridesmaids' dresses. Beautiful flowers for a posy include miniature and medium-sized roses, sweet peas, hyacinths, Queen Anne's lace, nerines, baby's breath and tiny carnations.

Bouquet Alternatives

There are no rules to dictate a bride's choice of bouquet and not all brides yearn for a traditional white bouquet. Since the 1960s more and more brides have chosen unstructured less formal bouquets. With the wealth of floral material available, a bride may choose a bouquet consisting of carefree wildflowers, meaningful herbs, youthful daisies or colorful autumn foliage highlighted with vibrant berries.

A country wedding lends itself perfectly to less traditional flowers. A bride can take advantage of lovely local wildflowers or the abundance of cottage blooms available. Interesting grasses, foliage, woody capsules and decorative fruits might be considered for a bouquet and look wonderful decorating a romantic stone church. Cheerful daffodils, mimosa, sunflowers and snapdragons all provide colorful country charm.

Herbal Bouquet

A fragrant herbal bouquet will add a medieval touch to an old world wedding. In olden times these bouquets were known as tussie-mussies or nosegays and were carried to ward off diseases. Later on they were used to convey a message of love. Often an herbal bouquet bears a message from The Language of Flowers, see page 58.

Rosemary, the emblem of love and symbol of remembrance has always been considered a wedding herb. One of King Henry VIII's more fortunate wives, Anne of Cleves, wore a coronet of gold and precious stones entwined with rosemary. A sprig of rosemary in a bride's bouquet was considered an omen of a happy marriage.

An herbal bouquet is made of both leaves and blossoms arranged artistically for color and form. Lavender, chive flowers, violets, one or more rosebuds, forget-me-nots and honeysuckle are perfect flowers for an herbal bouquet. Artemisia, bay laurel,

rosemary, sage, variegated pineapple mint and scented geranium leaves all have fragrant and decorative foliage.

Autumn Bouquet

When we think of autumn, we visualize the magnificent colors of deciduous shrubs and trees. When flowers are few, colorful autumn foliage could be used as a feature in a bridal bouquet and as decoration for the ceremony and reception. The various tones of the Japanese maple make a striking outline to a bouquet containing coral-colored roses. Chrysanthemums are plentiful in autumn and their russet tones are perfect with colored foliage. Bright red berries are also in abundance and make a memorable bouquet, floral bracelet and headpiece when teamed with variegated leaves or silver eucalyptus foliage. Exaggerated arrangements of colorful autumn foliage and boughs of berries could carry the theme through to the ceremony and reception. Rose hips are also very decorative.

Winter Bouquet of Dried Flowers

While fresh flowers offer fragrance, dried flowers will be a blessing for the winter bride when little else is available. They can also be retained for years and make a pleasing memento. Modern dried flowers come in many glorious vibrant colors as well as in pretty pastels. They are available year-round regardless of season or country of origin and you will have a far greater variety to choose from than you would of flowers fresh from the florist.

Grasses, seed pods and berries can also be dried and many wildflowers dry beautifully. You will be able to select floral material to create a particular theme or to suit a special color combination.

A florist will be able to make a bridal bouquet with dried flowers in any bouquet shape you choose from a loose bouquet to be cradled in the arms, to a tight Victorian posy. Dried flowers are particularly useful in headpieces, which require sturdy flowers that won't wilt.

Pressed Flowers from a Bouquet

Many brides keep their bouquets for pressing or to save for someone special, such as a relative or friend unable to attend the wedding. Rather than toss the bridal bouquet to the assembled young women at the reception, it is possible to have a smaller version of the bouquet made up by the florist for this purpose. It is also possible to have a small section of the bouquet made removable, so that it can be tossed to the young women gathered, or so it may be made into a corsage to be worn on the bride's going-away outfit, allowing her to throw the rest of the bouquet.

Pressing flowers is an art, but it is not difficult to achieve good results. The easiest flowers to press are those that can be pressed whole, such as delphiniums, pansies and sweet peas. Flowers with thick heads, such as roses and carnations, will need to have their petals separated before pressing. Detached petals are reassembled later when completely dried. Trumpet-shaped flowers such as daffodils, hyacinth and freesia are sliced in half lengthwise. Thick flowers in bud are unsuitable for pressing.

Flowers should be pressed as soon as possible after the day of the wedding. If you are unable to do this, it might be best to ask someone to do it for you. Never spray the bouquet with water — the surface of the flowers should be completely dry. Choose flowers that are undamaged and press more than you think you will need. Do not forget

to press any ferns and foliage from your bouquet. Always press plant parts of equal thickness together and do not allow any plant material to overlap.

You may wish to use a special flower press, or you can use heavy books. Sheets of blotting paper folded in half are recommended for pressing flowers in books. Arrange flowers and foliage on one half of the blotting paper and fold the other half over. Close the book and weigh it down with other heavy books. Leave the flowers undisturbed for six weeks. The longer they remain in the press, the better they will hold their color.

Arrange your pressed flowers in a floral scene that best resembles your bouquet. If this does not work, move the flowers around until a pleasing grouping falls into place. It is easiest to work with the foliage first and make arrangements from flowers that have been pressed whole. Finally, reassemble flowers with detached petals. When you are completely satisfied with the grouping, lift each piece carefully and apply glue with a fine paintbrush. Use a clear glue and take care as the fragile flower parts tend to break easily. You might find it easier to handle the petals with tweezers. The final result should be placed under a sheet of glass as soon as possible.

Take your finished picture to a professional framer, who will advise you on a suitable mount and help you with your choice of frame.

Bridesmaids and Flower Girls

The choice of style, color and flowers in bridesmaids' bouquets is virtually unlimited; the only consideration is that they should suit the setting and should not be so elaborate that they overshadow the bride's bouquet.

Whether the bouquets of the bridesmaids are of a style similar to the bride's is a matter of personal choice. When chosen with an eye to the total bridal color scheme, vibrant color can be introduced into a bridesmaid's bouquet. All the bridesmaids' bouquets do not necessarily have to be of the same color or flower but they will work best if they are of the same style. A clever florist should be able to create individual

bouquets but still maintain harmony in color, choice of ribbon and foliage.

If the bride's attendants are young, the flowers can be carefree, dainty and expressive of youth. If the bride wishes to evoke a period by for example carrying a Victorian posy, the theme can be continued in the bridesmaids' and flowergirls' bouquets. Often a posy is the most favored for bridesmaids. It is both romantic and elegant and can be carried by an attendant of any age.

Prayer books decorated with a trailer of flowers are also popular for bridesmaids. A very beautiful fragrant

There are many styles and shapes of baskets available and the florist will match the floral arrangement to suit the shape. The choice of size should be kept in proportion to the age and size of the attendants. For a young flower girl, a small basket is best filled with small flowers such as pinks, sweet peas, hyacinths, miniature roses, tiny daisies, baby's breath and Queen Anne's lace. A garden basket with open sides that allow flowers to flow out either side is more suited to an older and taller bridesmaid.

Floral Necklace

For a spring country wedding a fresh floral necklace made with daffodils, jonquils, hyacinth florets and roses will look beautiful on bridesmaids. Wildflowers also look good made into necklaces. Small attendants could wear floral bracelets to match.

winter trailer could be made using hellebores, violets and daphne.

Flower Baskets

If you have very young attendants, you may prefer that they carry baskets of fresh flowers rather than bouquets. Baskets of flowers can also look very effective when carried by older bridesmaids and a bride may also choose to carry a basket at a country-style wedding.

Headpieces

Bridesmaids and flower girls often wear flowers as headdresses. A headband worn across the head from ear to ear will suit almost any bridesmaid. Small circlets of myrtle leaves with just a few flowers added are lovely for small flower girls.

No matter which headpiece you choose, it is a good idea for you and your attendants to practise turning and bending while wearing your headpieces before the wedding ceremony.

Floral Ball

A small floral ball hanging from the wrist on a loop of ribbon is particularly suitable for a young child attendant. A floral ball is made of plastic foam covered with fresh flowers. Sturdy, rounded flowers such as small carnations, everlasting daisies, pompom dahlias and tiny chrysanthemums are ideal for arranging on a floral ball. More delicate flowers run the risk of being damaged during the event.

Boutonnieres

The groom, best man, groomsmen, bride's father and groom's father all wear flower boutonnieres in their left lapel. Men's boutonnieres are most often made with one flower or one flower and a bud and foliage. Carnations, gardenias, azaleas, roses and camellias are among those flowers chosen to be used as boutonnieres. Traditionally only white flowers were used, but a bride may prefer a color chosen to match the bridal bouquet. The groom generally wears a different flower from those of the other men. For him the most beautiful example found in the bridal bouquet would be perfect.

It is the job of the best man to ensure the boutonnieres are in place. They should always be positioned with the stalk of the flower pointing downward. It is best not to force a boutonniere into a buttonhole that is too small. Instead use a long florist's pin with a bead head and pass the point of the pin from the back of the lapel. The point goes over the stem just under the flower head and back through the fabric. The pin may need to be bent a little so that the lapel lies flat.

Corsages

It is customary for the groom to send corsages to his mother and the bride's mother and sometimes to other female relatives.

The wearing of a corsage is a matter of personal preference, and it is best to check first with the people involved before ordering the flowers. If a corsage is to be worn, it is important to find out what colors they will be wearing before choosing the flowers. Sometimes a woman may prefer to wear her corsage attached to her handbag. If it is not possible to establish the color of each person's outfit, it is best to choose neutral shades that are unlikely to clash. Gardenias, roses, orchids and camellias are good choices for the bride's and the groom's mother as they go well with most outfits. Ribbons and ferns are often included in corsages and should also be chosen so that they harmonize with the clothes of the wearer.

The shape of a corsage is usually elongated, with the flower stem forming a slender handle bound with florist's tape. Corsages worn on the shoulder are always pinned into position with the stems pointing upward.

≈ *Flowers for the Ceremony* ≈

It is essential that you visit the place where the wedding is to take place before planning the flower arrangements.

Consult with officials at the ceremony about where flowers can be placed. For example, you will need to check whether it is appropriate to put flowers on a church altar.

Find out whether there will be another wedding on that day. It may be possible to share the flowers and the costs.

If friends or members of your family are to arrange the flowers, it will be necessary to find out what pedestals and containers are available. This way you can decide upon the size and number of flowers needed.

The flowers for the ceremony are generally coordinated with the flowers carried by the bridal party. The mood or architecture of the building, however, may mean it will require special treatment. The interiors of some churches for example, are heavily paneled with wood and may be somewhat dark. Yellow and white flowers add light and beauty to a dim atmosphere. A large church with a high ceiling needs tall flower arrangements. A very modern church can take flowers with bold lines, such as lilies, agapanthus and tulips.

Cottage garden flowers or wildflowers are ideal for a small country church, while a very ornate church would look beautiful with full-blown garden roses. Camellias with their own lovely leaves, and chrysanthemums, azaleas and rhododendrons with their flowing lines would also be suitable.

If the bridal party is to carry or wear elaborate masses of flowers, then the most effective decoration at the ceremony may simply be a few arrangements of foliage and a vase or two of flowers. If in a church a pair of vases is to be placed on either side of

the altar, the arrangements should be identical. Other suitable places for floral decoration in a church might be smaller arrangements in the recesses of windows, a large arrangement on pedestals on either side of the chancel steps, welcoming displays at the entrance and pew decorations. Even in a small church, arrangements will need to contain some bold varieties in order to be seen from some distance.

Consider using flowering plants in pots as floral decoration instead of cut flowers. These would look particularly good at the entrance and might includes pots of azaleas, hydrangeas or miniature roses.

Pew Decorations

Small arrangements at the aisle end of the pews can be very effective at a wedding. They may consist of a posy of flowers tied with a white ribbon, a cascade of ivy, a small wreath of myrtle leaves decorated with a few fragrant flowers or a bunch of white, fresh or paper daisies. If you want the ends of the pews decorated, you will need to make a special note on the shape of the ends and the possibilities for attaching decorations.

Elegant arum lilies with white trailing ribbons make fashionable pew-end decorations. They are, however, quite tall and must be secured fairly low down as they will obstruct the view for some people and run the risk of being knocked over by people taking their places. Pew decorations need not be elaborate and should be small enough to allow easy access for guests entering the pew. They also should not be too wide, especially if the church has a narrow aisle.

The flowers should be chosen for their ability to survive for several hours out of water and remain looking fresh. If the wedding is to be held in midsummer, it might be worthwhile considering dried flowers or at least those that dry well; for example, statice, everlasting daisies and lavender. A charming, long-lasting pew decoration can be made using silver eucalyptus foliage, baby's breath, dried honesty and silver everlasting daisies secured in hanging bunches and tied with a generous bow of white tulle.

The essence of spring can be captured with the fragrance of flowering bulbs decorating each pew end. Lily of the valley, hyacinth, jonquils and freesias tied with ribbons matching the bridal theme will fill the church with their own special perfume.

≈ RECEPTION FLOWERS ≈

Flowers can be used to set the mood of your chosen theme for the reception. This could be a color link with the flowers chosen for the ceremony, a stylistic color scheme such as an all-green-and-white theme, or a flamboyant color combination using flowers and table linen in harmonious lipstick shades.

Flowers should be concentrated in places most likely to be viewed by the guests when either standing or sitting. In most instances flower arrangements are best placed high up to be fully appreciated. Borrow or consider hiring flower pedestals if the reception is to be held in a large area.

If you are holding your reception at a restaurant, hotel or in reception rooms, the flowers are often part of the package deal. You will need to check with the banquet manager that the flowers will harmonize with your color theme and style of wedding. Some establishments will have no objection if you wish to make the flower arrangements yourself.

If the reception is to be held at the bride's home, the floral decoration needs to be bold in order to transform a domestic setting into an atmosphere of celebration. For a home wedding avoid small vases of flowers placed here and there because they will not be noticed. The most effective way to decorate the interior of a house is to have large arrangements of flowers, boughs of blossoms and any attractive

greenery you can find. Have at least one stunning arrangement at the entrance near the receiving line, one where the photographs are to be taken and one as a centerpiece on a buffet table. Don't forget to place flowers where the speeches are to be given and where the cake is to be cut. Leave room for guests to circulate and position arrangements where they won't get knocked over.

Decorating a large reception hall or tent is very time-consuming and could be very expensive. Here again you will need flamboyant arrangements for impact. You will probably need to supply your own vases, containers and pedestals. Use the biggest you can find. Pickings from gardens can work wonders and might include daisies, roses, chrysanthemums, azaleas, rhododendrons, hydrangeas and large branches of blossoms or decorative foliage. When flowers are few, consider branches of fruit trees with their fruit attached, such as lemons, apples, pears and blueberries. Make large arrangements for the entrance, the stage, around the band, where the speeches are to be given and any other strategic points. Trails of ivy interspersed with white flowers are attractive as decoration for tent poles, the front of the stage, the bridal table and the table for the cake. To lessen the workload of the day, large garlands of dried flowers could be made up days in advance and fresh flowers used only for table decorations.

Flowers for the Tables

If people are to be seated at tables, fresh flowers will add greatly to the scene. Depending on the length and shape of the bridal table, there may be one large centerpiece or two or more smaller arrangements along the table. Although the flowers for the bridal table will be more elaborate than those for the guests' tables, they should not be so large as to hide the bridal couple from view.

The choice of flowers for table decorations will follow on from the style of the wedding and will play a supporting role in enhancing the mood. The color of the linen, china and containers should be chosen to harmonize with the color of the flowers. Every table decoration should be low enough for guests to be able to see one another. All sides of an arrangement will be seen, so it should be equally attractive from all angles.

Name cards on dining tables are given a special touch by the addition of an individual floral gift.

Buffet Tables

Sometimes the wedding cake may form the centerpiece for a buffet table, but more often it sits on its own table and the buffet table is decorated with flowers.

A floral arrangement on a buffet table should be higher than the level of the food and quite flamboyant. If the table is to be placed in the center of the room, the arrangement must be designed to look attractive from all sides. Here the choice of container will echo the style of the wedding. A tall

and stately epergne would make a magnificent centerpiece for a formal wedding when filled with camellias, lilies and orchids. Crystal vases containing full-blown garden roses are perfect for a romantic wedding. A tall spaghetti jar will provide plenty of room for daisies and chrysanthemums and will give the decoration height, placing it well out of harm's way. A table for cocktail food might have a highly elegant vase filled with iris or tuberose, while a country table could have a large wicker basket filled with cottage flowers and herbs.

Instead of flowers, fruit can be used as a centerpiece for the buffet table. An exaggerated arrangement using a variety of seasonal fruits and berries is especially lovely for a cheese table.

Wedding Cake Decorations

Fresh flowers are sometimes preferred for the decoration of the wedding cake. Some wedding cakes will only have a tiny arrangement placed on top, while others may be festooned with flowers on every layer. A beautiful idea is to decorate each layer with tiny rosebuds and to place the cake on a silver tray completely covered with opened roses. A tiered wedding cake looks especially elegant decorated with sprays of white lilac and ivy.

A small arrangement of flowers for the cake top is often made with the same variety of flowers used in the bride's bouquet. It can be made as a flat posy to sit flush on the top of the cake or arranged to resemble flowers in a vase. A small silver vase is ideal for carrying a posy of flowers, but it must be in proportion to the cake or it will make the cake look top-heavy. To avoid accidents, never put water in the vase and ensure that it is held firmly in place.

If using fresh flowers, wait until the last possible moment before putting them into position as they could wilt quickly in warm weather. Do not forget to have extra flowers or foliage for the base. Suitable flowers might include a scattering of violets, miniature carnations or roses, florets of hyacinths or stephanotis, sprigs of lilac or baby's breath. Rose leaves, ferns, ivy, myrtle and camellia leaves are all excellent as foliage decoration.

III

≈ WEDDING FEASTS ≈

≈ WEDDING FEASTS ≈

≈ PLANNING ≈

*F*or centuries the traditonal way to celebrate a wedding has been by sharing food and wine. The wedding reception has become one of life's celebrations and can vary from a glass of champagne and a few canapés to an elaborate sit-down meal with fine wines served by a plethora of waiters.

The availability of many new and unusual venues, plus stylish party accessories for rent and an increasing number of imaginative caterers, makes planning a wedding feast exciting and fun.

The type of food served at the reception will be influenced by the time of day, the size of the wedding, the space and facilities where the party is to be held and the budget. Whatever the type of food offered, it should be fresh, of the best quality and the presentation should be excellent. Since the day is intended to be memorable, there should be at least one inventive or extravagant offering.

Deciding The Venue

You may hold your reception at home, at a hotel, restaurant, club, reception center, hall or in a tent. Your choice may be governed by the number of guests, your budget and the style of wedding you would like to have. In order to take the worry out of catering a wedding party, many brides choose a hotel or reception center where they can depend on professional advice and service.

Many reception centers are experienced in catering for weddings and will work out a package deal to meet your individual requirements. This might include pre-dinner drinks, sit-down dinner or buffet with wine and champagne. The banquet manager will help you choose a suitable menu and appropriate wines. You will need to discuss the color scheme for the tables and determine the seating arrangements.

Often there will be a list of optional extras such as wedding cake, flowers, photographer, musicians and a room in which to change. Some hotels offer a bridal suite with complimentary champagne waiting.

Often a bride will choose her favorite restaurant knowing that the food and service will be everything she would wish for her guests. Many restaurants cater large or small scale receptions depending on the space available. Most are happy to work out a tailor-made menu to suit your style of wedding and the time of day.

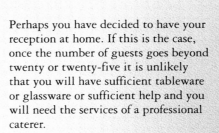

When choosing a hotel, reception rooms or restaurant not personally known to you, it is a good idea to order a meal there beforehand to get some idea of their standards and presentation. It might be necessary to shop around, get quotes and compare services before making a definite booking.

Perhaps you have decided to have your reception at home. If this is the case, once the number of guests goes beyond twenty or twenty-five it is unlikely that you will have sufficient tableware or glassware or sufficient help and you will need the services of a professional caterer.

If you decide to hold your reception in a hall, thought must be given to kitchen facilities and equipment. You will probably need to hire an outside caterer. Many good catering companies have excellent portable heating equipment and will transport food and drinks in refrigerated trucks. Some will just attend to the food while others will take care of all the arrangements for you. Here again, shop around as there is a considerable variation in price and services available.

Multiple Food Stations

For a large wedding it is a good idea to prepare separate food stations. This will avoid long lines at the buffet table and enable guests to wander happily and mingle well around the tables.

Food stations work particularly well at an outdoor reception where different foods can be served in special locations, such as under a romantic shady tree, against an old stone wall or from a leafy conservatory. If renting a large tent, consider having several smaller tents. Food can be adapted to the season, budget, number of staff, space and taste. The following are a few ideas for separate food stations.

Oyster and Shellfish Bar

Serve from large beds of ice. Decorate with branches of lemons, limes and ferns. Have on hand aromatic fennel, dill and good quality lemons, seafood sauces and triangle sandwiches. You will need large quantities of ice. Plan for running water and some drainage. Provide attractive disposal bins for shells.

Serve:
Bowl of caviar on ice, with lemon wedges and toast triangles
Platter of large prawns
Lobster cut in slices and replaced in shells
Steamed mussels piled on large cake stand
Oysters on the half shell served from a giant clam shell
Selection of seafood sauces

Carving Table

You may want to hire a professional chef to carve the meat and you will need an experienced person to serve. Plan for heating devices.

Serve:
Hot rare roast beef and horseradish dressing
Whole suckling pig
Turkey with ham and apricot seasoning
Crispy roast potatoes and rosemary
Green beans and zesty sauce
Glazed julienne parsnips and carrots
Hot herb bread

Salad Bar

A self-serve salad bar will need one person in attendance to replace platters and bowls as they empty. Decorate the bar with wild flowers or colorful garden flowers or an elaborate vegetable arrangement.

Serve:
Wild rice and brown rice salad
Tomato and basil salad
Waldorf salad
Pasta salad
Mixed green salad and herbs
Mushroom salad
Three-bean salad
Potato salad with basil or mint dressing
Spinach salad with pine nut dressing

Barbecue

The barbecue area needs to be some distance from the main wedding party. You will need two experienced cooks.

Serve:
Racks of lamb
Lamb kebabs
Chicken drumsticks with basil butter
Satay chicken with peanut sauce
Marinated barbecue beef
Glazed pork spareribs

Cheese Table

This table can be self-serve. The cheeses will need to be replenished as needed and occasionally 'tidied.' Serve a variety of cheeses with assorted breads and crackers in baskets. Decorate with grape leaves and tiers of colorful fruit.

Beverage Bar

Cover the bar table with a large white tablecloth reaching to the floor to hide extra bottles and stored ice. You will need one bartender for every fifty to seventy-five people.

Wedding Cake Table

The wedding cake table should be covered with the most beautiful cloth you can find. Decorate it with romantic roses, elegant lilies or dainty cottage flowers. Allow easy access for guests to gather for the cake-cutting ceremony.

≈ CELEBRATION IDEAS ≈

Morning Wedding

A morning wedding party is perfect for the couple that has made travel arrangements for the early part of the day. The food can be light and simple, this will also help keep costs down. The bridal party and the immediate family can follow up the reception with a celebratory lunch.

The following suggested menu can be served buffet style and is easy to manage at a standing reception.

MENU
Mini vol-au-vents filled with seafood
Cherry tomatoes filled with pesto
Finger sandwiches with herb butters and dainty fillings
Small crepes with a selection of sweet or savory fillings
Smoked eel pâté served with hot brioche

Assorted sweet pastries
Basket of fresh strawberries
Wedding cake

Tea and coffee

Wine and champagne

A Wedding At Noon

A cold buffet lunch is particularly suitable for a large wedding. There is only one course for this meal. The hors d'oeuvres are served as an appetizer. The food is laid out on a buffet table in the order in which it is to be eaten. Guests pick up their plates, help themselves to the food and finally pick up cutlery and napkins. Wine is passed around on a tray. Small tables and chairs should be available so that older guests may sit down.

The following suggested menu is easy to serve and the food can be eaten standing up.

MENU
Button mushrooms stuffed with pâté
and chopped walnuts
Cherry tomatoes filled with caviar

Stuffed grape leaves
Tortellini salad
Ratatouille
Mini crepes with filling of your choice
Fresh asparagus with watercress
cream dip
Fillet of beef salad
Seafood salad
Garden salad

Wedding cake
Tea and coffee

Chilled white wine and champagne

QVB

Nicole and David's Wedding Dinner
at the Queen Victoria Ballroom

Canapes
Chicken lotus blossoms
Smoked salmon crepes
Trout Pate on heart shaped croutons

Rolls and butter

Entree
Cured Atlantic salmon served with a dill cream

Main Course
Chick... ...tuffed with oyster mushroom and a green peppercorn
sauce
...ed with a selection of seasonal vegetables
Heart shaped white chocolate nougat mousse with raspberry couli and

Dessert
fresh raspberries

Cheese
King Island brie and water crackers
Pears, grapes and fresh dates

Coffee and chocolates

A Reception At Home For 50

A wedding reception in the home is friendly and affordable and will be a great success if you are very well organized.

Catering for a Crowd

The most important things that need to be considered are the space, the menu and the service. If space is limited in the home, it might be worth considering renting a tent and furniture. Professional caterers are often called in to help with large parties. They will take the worry out of cooking, provide the necessary tableware and continue the service by supplying the staff. If you decide to do your own catering, you will need to arrange for the rental of glasses, plates, cutlery and table linens. If kitchen space and time are limited, consider having one part of the meal catered, such as the hors d'oeuvres or the desserts.

You will need assistance with the preparation, serving and cleaning up. You will need at least three people to help on the day and it is wise to hire the services of staff from a catering company. Fifty people can make a lot of mess, and you do not want your guests in their best clothes clearing tables and washing up.

It is unwise to provide a serve yourself bar for a crowd. This will lead to a greater consumption of alcohol than if drinks are circulated on a tray served by a bartender.

The easiest way of catering is to serve the meal from a buffet table placed in the middle of the room so that guests can walk around the table, the wedding cake on a table of its

own. Seasonings, sauces, cutlery, napkins and bread rolls can be placed on the guests' tables. This will save a great deal of time and congestion at the buffet table, and guests will be seated more quickly.

Table Arrangements

The suggested menu on page 100 consists of hors d'oeuvres to be passed around with pre-dinner drinks, and a hot buffet. Ideally, for the type of food suggested, guests should be able to sit at a table. If you have a large living room, rent round tables and cafe chairs and set them up restaurant-style. Other places to consider for tables and chairs are a conservatory, an enclosed verandah or a family room. If the weather is pleasant, a patio or enclosed courtyard might be suitable. A tent will shelter guests and food from the weather and will provide plenty of space for the buffet and dining tables. Linen can be rented or borrowed, but make sure you know the table sizes so that the tablecloths fit perfectly. Choose tablecloths and napkins in colors that blend with your overall scheme.

Place Cards

Regardless of the number of guests, if there is to be a sit-down meal, it will be necessary to have a seating plan and place cards. At a large wedding it is usual to have the seating plan conveniently displayed advising guests of their table number. If there are place cards on the table, guests will quickly find their seats without difficulty.

Planning Ahead

When catering for a wedding, it is essential to have most of the preparation done beforehand. The success of the day will depend on delegation of work, borrowing or renting to supplement existing equipment and attention to detail. Plan the menu ahead and make a work schedule. Write shopping lists well in advance. Keep a main list of each of the things you are going to do in the order you intend to do them.

Don't prepare too much food, since these days people do not want or expect huge amounts. People tend to help themselves to a little of each dish offered in preference to making a meal of one. Remember that you do not need to allow one portion of everything for each guest. Microwave ovens are very portable, so borrow a few to help with the reheating.

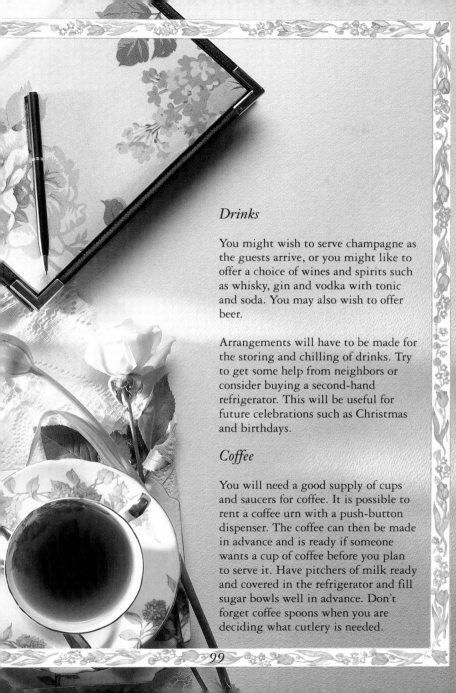

Drinks

You might wish to serve champagne as the guests arrive, or you might like to offer a choice of wines and spirits such as whisky, gin and vodka with tonic and soda. You may also wish to offer beer.

Arrangements will have to be made for the storing and chilling of drinks. Try to get some help from neighbors or consider buying a second-hand refrigerator. This will be useful for future celebrations such as Christmas and birthdays.

Coffee

You will need a good supply of cups and saucers for coffee. It is possible to rent a coffee urn with a push-button dispenser. The coffee can then be made in advance and is ready if someone wants a cup of coffee before you plan to serve it. Have pitchers of milk ready and covered in the refrigerator and fill sugar bowls well in advance. Don't forget coffee spoons when you are deciding what cutlery is needed.

Wedding Menu for 50 guests
Self Catered in Your Home

Cheddar straws and Parmesan rounds
Salmon pâté with melba toasts
Finger sandwiches — three layered

Buffet
Honey glazed leg of ham served with spiced cherries
Apple and tarragon stuffed chicken breast
Fillet of beef tenderloin with a horseradish cream

Mixed leaf green salad
Sliced tomato with fresh basil
New potato salad with sour cream, fresh dill and chives
Cob loaves, French loaves
Crocks of butter

Tira mi su
(Italian layered chocolate pudding)
Bowl of whole strawberries marinated in Port

Coffee and Wedding cake

Cheddar Straws

1 packet frozen puff pastry sheets
250 g (8 oz) cheddar cheese, grated
3 egg yolks, beaten
sesame seeds

Cut pastry into strips approximately 8cm (3") long and 2 cm (3/4") wide. Brush with beaten egg. Sprinkle cheese over the top pressing down slightly. Take both ends and twist in opposite directions to curl. Bake in a moderate oven for 8 minutes or until golden. Yields 80.

Parmesan Rounds

160 g (6 oz) plain (all-purpose) flour
1/2 tsp baking powder
250 g (8 oz) Parmesan cheese, grated
125 g (4 oz) butter
1/4 tsp cayenne

Sift the dry ingredients into a bowl with the cheese. Rub in the butter then add one egg and a little water if too dry. Shape into a roll 38 cm (15") long. Refrigerate for 3 hours. Remove and slice roll into 7 mm (1/4") rounds. Bake for 15 minutes in a moderate oven until golden brown. Yields 80.

Salmon Pâté with Melba Toasts

Salmon pâté
(Prepare up to 3 days before)
2 x 440 g (14 oz) cans red salmon
375 g (12 oz) cream cheese
3 tbsp lemon juice
3 tbsp horseradish sauce
6 tbsp shallots (scallions), finely chopped
1 bunch dill, chopped
Blend salmon, cream cheese, lemon juice and horseradish sauce in a food processor until smooth. Add shallots (scallions) and dill. Spoon into decorative bowls, cover and refrigerate.

Melba Toasts
(Prepare up to one week before)
With an electric knife cut thin slices from a chilled baguette loaf of bread and place on a baking tray. Bake in a moderate oven until golden brown. Cool and store in an airtight container.

Three Layered Ribbon Sandwiches

Bread
Order 3 loaves of brown and 3 loaves of white bread and have the bread put through the slicer length ways. This will give you about 6 to 7 slices. Assemble three slices of bread in alternate colors. Butter the bread. The center slice should be buttered on both sides. Put fillings in that will complement each other in taste, texture and color. Wrap the

sandwiches in damp tea towels, then wrap in cling plastic wrap and refrigerate. About 2 hours before serving trim the crust from the sandwiches with an electric knife and slice into slim fingers about 2.5 cm (1") wide. Arrange on a silver tray or a shallow wicker basket and decorate with fresh flowers. Cover with a damp tea towel and keep in a cool place.

Fillings
Make the fillings in advance and choose fillings that are firm and easy to eat (not sloppy).
Suggested fillings: leg ham with seeded mustard, diced chicken with mayonnaise and fresh mint, smoked turkey breast with cranberry sauce, smoked salmon, thinly sliced rare beef with mango chutney, mashed egg mayonnaise with fresh chives, cucumber, alfalfa, watercress.
Avoid: shredded lettuce, tomato, beetroot, onion.

Buffet

Honey Glazed Leg of Ham
(Prepare the day before)

Order a 10 to 12 kg (22 to 26 lb) cooked leg ham which will give you 50 generous serves.
Remove the thick skin from the ham with a sharp knife leaving the skin on the shank of the ham. Cut a diamond pattern into the fat about 2.5 cm (1") deep and stud the center of each diamond with a whole clove. Mix a thick paste of honey and brown sugar and rub onto the ham.

Line a large baking dish with foil and place the ham on it. Cook the ham at 150°C (300°F) until the fat is golden brown. Baste with honey paste while cooking. The ham can be served warm or cold depending on the weather. Place it on a large platter and decorate by tying a ham frill and a white satin bow around the shank.

Spiced Black Cherry Sauce

500 ml (17 fl oz) water
500 ml (17 fl oz) white wine
8 tbsp red wine vinegar
4 sticks of cinnamon
12 whole cloves
16 tbsp sugar
2 tbsp orange rind julienned
4 cans of pitted black cherries

Boil together water, white wine, red wine vinegar, cinnamon, cloves and sugar. Reduce this mixture until thick by boiling hard. Add orange rind and drained black cherries. Serve either hot or cold.

Apple and Tarragon Stuffed Chicken Breasts
(Prepare the day before)

Order 40 fillets of chicken with the skin still on.

Apple stuffing
Peel and dice 20 cooking apples into 12 mm (1/2") dice. In a large pan add 250 g (8 oz) of butter and sauté the diced apple. While cooking sprinkle with salt, ground pepper and finely chopped fresh tarragon. Do not overcook, the texture must be still firm. Cool.

To stuff the fillets
Form a pocket under the skin by gently pushing your fingers between the skin and the flesh of chicken. Do not force too near the sides as it will pull the skin completely away from the breast. Put approximately 2 tbsp of the apple mixture into the pocket you have formed.

Tuck each end of the breast over and place close together in a baking dish so they don't lose their shape. Brush the breasts with melted butter and bake for about 15 minutes at 180°C (350°F) until cooked.

Refrigerate until ready to serve. Two hours prior to serving, cut each breast crosswise into 3 or 4 slices and layer onto a large platter to reveal the stuffing. Cover with cling plastic wrap and refrigerate. Garnish at the last moment with fresh tarragon.

Fillet of Beef Tenderloin with Horseradish Cream

Order 5 trimmed and tied tenderloin fillets of beef approximately 2.5 kg (5 1/2 lb) each. This is allowing approximately 200 g (7 oz) per person. For a cheaper cut suitable for baking, use scotch fillet or sirloin plate.

Before baking rub crushed peppercorns or herbs of Provence into the beef. In a baking dish put 2 tbsp of oil and heat to a high temperature. Brown the fillets all over. Transfer the beef to a very hot oven 250°C (475°F) and cook for 25 minutes. Cool, remove the string and wrap in aluminium foil and refrigerate until ready to serve.

About 2 hours before, slice the fillets 7mm (1/4") thick (you should get 12 slices from each fillet) overlap on a large platter. Cover with cling plastic wrap and refrigerate. At the last

moment garnish with fresh herbs and flowers.

Horseradish cream
Mix 2 x 300 g (9 1/2 oz) cartons of sour cream with a 150 g (5 oz) jar of horseradish sauce to taste and serve separately in a sauce boat.

Mixed Leaf Green Salad

Buy a selection of lettuce —
mignonette, cos, frizzie, raddichio and
selected herbs — watercress, Italian
parsley, coriander. Calculate about
3 leaves per person.

The day before: Wash and dry the
lettuce, count the leaves and put into
plastic bags, tie up and mark on the
bag the number of serves and
refrigerate until needed.

*An easy way to dry a large quantity of
lettuce leaves is to put the wet leaves
into a clean pillow slip and spin dry on
a short spin cycle in your washing
machine.

Green Salad Vinaigrette
(Prepare up to one week ahead)

4 tbsp Dijon Mustard
4 cloves garlic
1 tbsp cracked pepper
500 ml (16 fl oz) vegetable oil
180 ml (6 fl oz) white vinegar
3 tbsp brown sugar

Blend all ingredients together in a
food processor. Put in a jar and
refrigerate.

Tomato Salad with Fresh Basil Vinaigrette

Slice 25 medium sized tomatoes and
arrange on a large flat platter. Sprinkle
with chopped fresh basil, cover with
cling plastic wrap and refrigerate for 2
hours. To serve, dress with a basil
vinaigrette.

Basil Vinaigrette
(Prepare up to 2 days before)

3 tbsp brown sugar
3 tsp Dijon or French mustard
1 tbsp cracked pepper
500 ml (16 fl oz) vegetable oil
1 bunch fresh basil
180 ml (6 fl oz) white vinegar

Combine sugar, mustard, pepper and
1/4 of the oil in a blender or food
processor. Add the basil leaves and
blend until the mixture is quite green.
Blend in the rest of the oil and vinegar,
transfer to a jar. Refrigerate. The
vinaigrette will retain its color for two
days.

Potato Salad with Sour Cream, Fresh Dill and Chives
(Prepare the day before)

25 medium potatoes
1 bunch mint
250 ml (8 fl oz) vinaigrette
3 x 300 g (9 1/2 oz) cartons sour cream
salt
black pepper
1 bunch chives
2 bunches dill
10 rashers bacon

Boil potatoes in salted water with a
bunch of fresh mint. While warm
remove the skins and slice into 7 mm
(1/4") slices. Sprinkle with vinaigrette
and cover with cling plastic wrap.

About 2 hours before: Beat sour cream
to a pouring consistency, then gently
fold it through the sliced potatoes.
Season with salt and freshly ground
black pepper, add the finely chopped
chives and one bunch of finely
chopped dill. Dice the bacon and fry in
a pan until brown. Spoon the potato
salad into a deep bowl and garnish
with the cooked bacon and the second
bunch of chopped fresh dill.

Tira Mi Su
(Prepare one day before)

5 x 250 g (8 oz) blocks of dark
(semi-sweet) chocolate
20 egg yolks
10 tbsp of castor sugar
vanilla to taste
750 g (24 oz) sour cream
150 g (5 oz) cream cheese
6 cups (1400 ml, 48 fl oz) fresh strong
coffee
70 sponge finger biscuits (ladyfingers)
15 x 250 g (8 oz) punnets of raspberries or
strawberries

Cut up the chocolate and melt in a
bowl over a saucepan of hot water, set
aside to cool. Beat the egg yolks with
the sugar and vanilla until the mixture
has trebled in size and is quite pale.
Mix the sour cream and cream cheese
and combine with the egg yolk
mixture. Dip the sponge fingers
(ladyfingers) in cold coffee just to coat
them — they should not become
soggy. Drain the sponge fingers
(ladyfingers) on kitchen paper.

Place a row of sponge fingers
(ladyfingers) on the base of a large
platter or ceramic serving dish.
Combine cooled chocolate with the
egg yolk mixture. Beat egg whites
until they hold soft peaks and gently
fold into the chocolate mixture.
Sprinkle mashed raspberries or

strawberries over the sponge fingers
(ladyfingers) and cover with a layer of
the chocolate mixture. Place another
row of sponge fingers (ladyfingers) on
top and repeat the fruit and chocolate.
Dust with cocoa and refrigerate.
You may have to make this dessert in 2
or 3 separate dishes depending on the
size of your containers.

Strawberries Marinated in Port

12 x 250 g (8 oz) punnets of strawberries
750 ml (24 fl oz) Port
375 g (12 oz) sugar
2 tsp powdered cinnamon
Wash and hull the strawberries. Boil
the rest of the ingredients rapidly until
sugar dissolves. Cool and pour over
strawberries.

An Afternoon-tea Wedding

An afternoon-tea wedding is romantic, and very elegant.

This is the simplest type of reception and can be easily catered at the bride's home after the ceremony. The menu should be carefully planned and as beautifully presented as possible.

This is a time for beautiful lace or antique tablecloths and gleaming silver. Bring out the fine bone china teacups. Lay out crystal sherry glasses and elegant champagne flutes to make the afternoon tea a true celebration.

Champagne is the traditional drink for weddings, but as Madeira and sherry team perfectly with a delicious afternoon feast, you may wish to break with tradition and keep the very best champagne for the toast.

Most of the food suggested can be cooked in advance, leaving only the sandwiches, garnishing and decorating to be done on the day.

Suggested Fillings for Finger Sandwiches

Cucumber and watercress
Avocado and bacon
Prawns and finely chopped celery
Leg ham and chutney
Egg and sliced stuffed olives
Steamed chicken and finely chopped shallots
Smoked salmon and finely chopped dill

MENU

Finger sandwiches
Iced eclairs
Pecan tartlets
Peach pie
Hazelnut cake with fresh raspberries
Viennese cookies
Marbled cheesecake

Wedding cake
Tea and coffee

Chilled sherry, Madeira and
champagne

Cocktail Party

Cocktail-party weddings are becoming
more and more popular and a cocktail
party is a relaxed and friendly way to
entertain a large number of people.
A variety of interesting finger food can
be served while guests mingle, chat
and sip chilled champagne. Prepare as
much food as possible in advance,
doing the final cooking just before
guests arrive.

Cocktail food is intended to stimulate
the appetite and is not a meal. Do not
be trapped into making the food too
ornate. All food should be in bite-sized
pieces that don't require a plate. A
good appetizer is only a mouthful.
Select a balance of vegetables, pâtés,
spicy foods, seafood, hot foods and
sensational sandwiches At a large party
ten to twelve varieties of appetizer
should be served. Depending on the
time of day, allow for three or four of
each variety per person.

Ideally cocktail food should be passed
on trays by waiters. If you plan to set
out a lavish buffet-style table so that
your guests can help themselves, do
not put out all the food at once, but
replenish platters often to keep the
food looking fresh. For every fifty
guests you will need at least one
bartender and one waiter.

Fresh Ideas for Hors D'oeuvres

Prosciutto-wrapped quartered figs
Prosciutto-wrapped melon
Prosciutto-wrapped strawberries
Profiteroles with a variety of
savory fillings
Blanched snow peas with
crab meat filling

≈ ≈ ≈

Mushroom caps stuffed with spinach
and prosciutto
Mushroom caps stuffed with crab
and pecan nuts
Herb sausage rolls cut into rounds
Shrimp wrapped in blanched snow
peas and secured with a toothpick
Chicken meatballs with oriental
dipping sauce

≈ ≈ ≈

Fresh asparagus with watercress
cream dip
Filo triangles with curried
chicken filling

New potatoes topped with
sour cream and caviar
Cherry tomatoes filled with pesto
Cherry tomatoes filled with blue
cheese and grated onion
Cherry tomatoes filled with bacon,
chopped shallots and
mayonnaise mixture

≈ ≈ ≈

Devilled eggs with black olives
Scallops marinated in lime juice and
wrapped in cucumber ribbons
Dates stuffed with blue Stilton and
chopped walnuts
Herb and garlic olives
Celery boats filled with green
peppercorn brie

Cocktail Canapés

Canapés take a little time to prepare, but look delicious when completed. A canapé is a platform or base topped with a savoury spread or pâté. You can cut canapés into any shape you wish, but they must be bite-sized and able to be eaten without utensils. Squares, diamonds and triangles do not waste any of the base ingredients, but heart-shaped bases are wonderful and romantic for a wedding.

The following make excellent bases for canapés:

Pumpernickel bread
French bread rounds
Mini toast
Rye bread
Sliced seedless cucumbers
Sliced medium-sized zucchini
Croutons

Serving Tips

Aim for elegant presentation and do not crowd each platter with food.

Make a soft bed of dill, watercress or lettuce on trays to prevent items such as eggs, potatoes and figs from rolling around.

Stuffed cherry tomatoes will not roll on a platter if you scoop out the bottoms and stand them stem-side down.

Tiny red cherry tomatoes make a colorful and edible garnish for platters.

≈ THE WEDDING CAKE ≈

The magnificent wedding cakes we have today go back to Roman times when the bride and groom partook in the eating of a humble cake made of flour and water.

The wedding cake is an essential part of the wedding celebration. It may be ordered from a caterer, a baker or a patisserie that specialises in wedding cakes. Hotels that cater for weddings will often provide a cake made by their own chefs.

Today the choice of wedding cake styles is wide. A bride will be able to choose from a variety of shapes, sizes, flavors, color schemes and decorations.

A wedding cake can be a five-tiered extravaganza of handmade sugar flowers and bows, or a small one-tiered cake topped with a posy of fresh flowers.

Skilled cake decorators will follow a wedding theme and take inspiration from the decoration or fabric of the bride's gown. Some will make icing flowers to match the flowers in the bridal bouquet. You may wish your florist to prepare a posy of fresh flowers for the top of the cake to match the bouquet. The most popular decoration for the top of the cake, of course, is a miniature bride and groom, available in a variety of styles through most bakers and caterers. Wedding bells are another favorite decoration.

It is wise to order the cake at least two months before the wedding. The average one tiered-cake serves about seventy people, a two-tiered cake serves 100 people; and a three-tiered cake serves up to 150 people. When ordering the cake, find out whether it will require a stand and if this will be supplied by the baker.

Remember to give some consideration to the knife for the cake-cutting ceremony. It must be large enough and suitable to cut the wedding cake, and should look attractive for the photographs. Many caterers will provide an appropriate ceremonial cake knife along with the other tableware.

The cutting of the cake is one of the highlights of the reception and marks the end of the meal and formalities.The bride places the point of the knife at the center of the bottom tier of the cake and the groom places his hand over hers. Together they cut the cake. If the cake is of a tricky nature, the first piece can be partly cut beforehand, but left in position for the bride and groom to finish cutting. The bride and groom feed each other the first mouthfuls of cake. The waiters then take the cake away to divide it into slices to hand around to the guests. Everyone present must partake of the bridal cake. It is considered unlucky for both the guest and the newlyweds if any guest does not eat the cake.

Traditionally absent friends and well-wishers are sent a small slice of the cake with a card in a small cardboard box. This is usually done by the bride's mother soon after the wedding.

The top tier of the wedding cake is traditionally kept for the couple to share on their first anniversary. Place the cake in a cardboard box, seal securely and store in the freezer.

≈ DRINKS AND NIBBLES ≈

Instead of the usual bowls of peanuts and potato chips, serve some of the following tasty nibbles.

Irresistible Nibbles

They can be passed around with cocktails or pre-dinner drinks or placed near the beverage bar. They can be prepared days in advance and will keep well for up to two weeks when stored in airtight containers.

SUGAR AND SPICE PECANS

500 g (1 lb) sugar
1 tsp salt
2 tbsp paprika
1 tsp cayenne pepper
1 tsp cumin powder
500 g (1 lb) shelled whole pecans
oil for frying

Place the sugar, salt, paprika, cayenne pepper and cumin in a bowl and mix well. In a large pot of boiling water, blanch the nuts for one minute. Remove with a strainer, drain and pat dry. Toss the nuts in the sugar and spice mixture.

In a deep saucepan, fry the nuts in hot oil until they turn golden brown. Remove them with a strainer and toss again in the sugar and spice mixture. Remove, shake off excess mixture and let cool on a wire rack. The nuts will turn crisp as they cool. Serve at room temperature.

GARLIC ALMONDS

2 tbsp soy sauce
2 tsp chili sauce
3 garlic cloves, crushed
500 g (1 lb) blanched almonds
salt and freshly ground white pepper

Grease a shallow baking pan with butter. In a bowl combine the soy sauce, chili sauce and garlic. Stir in the almonds until well coated. Place the almonds in the pan and sprinkle with a little salt and pepper. Bake in 350°F (180°C) oven for 10 minutes, then sprinkle with a little more salt and pepper if desired. Stir with a fork and bake 15 minutes more. Cool and store.

CINNAMON CASHEWS

185g (6 oz) salted roasted cashews
80 g (2 1/2 oz) sultanas (golden raisins)
1 tsp ground cinnamon
1 tsp oil

Heat the oil in frying pan, add the cashews and sultanas, and stir constantly over moderate heat for 2 minutes. Mix in the cinnamon. Drain and cool.

TOASTED CHICK PEAS

2 tbsp (30 ml) olive oil
2 cloves garlic, crushed
1 1/2 lb (750 g) chick peas, cooked and
drained
salt

Heat the oil in a large frying pan. Add
the garlic and chick peas. Cook gently
for about 5 minutes, stirring
frequently. Add the salt and stir
through.

Spread the chick peas evenly in a
shallow roasting pan. Toast in a
moderate oven for about 10 minutes or
until lightly browned. Turn during the
cooking. Serve warm.

SPICY BEER NUTS

2 cloves garlic, thinly sliced
2 cm (1") piece of ginger, slivered
250 g (8 oz) salted beer nuts
2 small dried chilies, crushed
oil

Heat a little oil in a frying pan and
sauté the garlic and ginger until
golden. Add the nuts and chilies and
sauté, stirring constantly, for 3
minutes. Drain and cool.

The Drinks Department

If you are having the reception in a hotel or reception hall, the manager will suggest which champagne and wines are the most suitable to be served as the guests arrive and during the meal. They usually charge only for the bottles actually opened.

At a reception at home you may wish to offer the guests a glass of fine sherry, white wine or champagne on their arrival. You may also provide beer, spirits, fruit juices, mixers and mineral water. A reputable wine merchant will usually arrange supplies on a sale or return basis and some will also lend glasses.

When calculating the number of drinks needed, it is important to err on the side of generosity. Estimate the amount of each type of drink you will need according to the number and preferences of your guests. The correct quantity is easy to calculate if you know that champagne or wine provides six glasses to the bottle, and spirits,

such as whisky, twenty-five drinks to the bottle. If you are serving a meal, calculate one bottle of wine or champagne per person. If you are having the full complement of toasts, make sure there is plenty of champagne to go around.

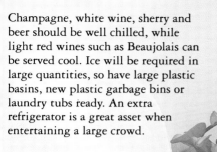

Champagne, white wine, sherry and beer should be well chilled, while light red wines such as Beaujolais can be served cool. Ice will be required in large quantities, so have large plastic basins, new plastic garbage bins or laundry tubs ready. An extra refrigerator is a great asset when entertaining a large crowd.

For a large, full-hearted wedding a beverage bar away from the workings of the kitchen is a necessity. Do try to have at least one bartender to operate the bar and if possible one or two waiters to circulate the drinks on a tray.

If a meal is served, the selection of wines depends on the menu. If more than one wine is to be served, remember that dry wines should be served before sweet, young wines before older wines, white before red, light-bodied before those with a fuller flavor, chilled wines before those served at room temperature, and sweet wines with sweet dishes.

Champagne

Champagne is the wine of celebrations
and the traditional wedding party
drink. It can be offered to guests as an
aperitif on their arrival at the reception
and, of course, as a toast. It also makes
a first-rate accompaniment to entrees
and cocktail food, and at some
weddings it is served throughout the
reception with mineral water and fresh
orange juice on the side. Always serve
champagne from tall narrow flutes as
they help trap all those delicious
bubbles.

Welcoming guests with a champagne
punch is a great idea. The following
recipe serves 15 to 20.

CHAMPAGNE PUNCH

375 ml (13 fl oz) brandy
500 ml (16 fl oz) dry white wine
100 ml (3 fl oz) Grand Marnier
1 orange, thinly sliced
1 lemon, thinly sliced
6 bottles of dry champagne, well chilled
1 (250 g, 8 oz) punnet fresh strawberries,
hulled and sliced
fresh mint sprigs

Combine the brandy, white wine,
Grand Marnier, and orange and lemon
slices in a bowl and allow to stand
overnight. Just before serving, strain
the mixture. Place ice blocks in a large
punch bowl and add the strained
mixture. Pour in the three bottles of
champagne. Add the sliced
strawberries and decorate with fresh
mint sprigs.

IV
≈ WEDDING IDEAS ≈

≈ WEDDING IDEAS ≈

≈ THE CEREMONY ≈

Every wedding is a very personal event. While many couples are rediscovering religious wedding traditions, others are transforming age-old customs into a personal expression of a commitment.

Personal Expressions

Individual circumstances will suggest either a religious or a civil ceremony, however a wedding ceremony is a time for expressing yourself in your own way, with the utmost honesty. You will be making very solemn vows about the way you intend to spend the rest of your life.

A church service can be varied to accommodate the couple's and the clergyman's views. For example, clergymen of all religions are willing to confront the times by omitting the word *obey* from the wedding vows. Because these vows are

considered very solemn and binding, very few brides promise to obey their husbands today. However if a couple chooses to be married using the lovely old Elizabethan words of the 1662 Book of Common Prayer, the promise by the bride to obey her husband is included.

It is also possible for a couple to select or write their own prayers in cooperation with the clergyman.

This is provided for by the Alternative Service Book 1980 which enables the man and woman to make equal promises and allows greater scope for those who wish to be unconventional.

Often couples wish to make a personal statement. This can be incorporated into the ceremony after the exchange of vows. Personal expressions might be in the form of a special prayer or a selected reading from the Bible. The following is a popular biblical reading adapted from 1 Corinthians:13 about the nature of love:

> Love is always patient and kind;
> It is never jealous;
> Love is never boastful or conceited;
> It is never rude or selfish;
> It does not take offense,
> And is not resentful.
>
> Love takes no pleasure
> In other people's faults
> But delights in the truth;
> It is always ready to excuse, to trust, to hope.
> It is always ready to endure whatever comes.
> True love does not come to an end.

Also from 1 Corinthians: 13 is this short passage:

> So faith, hope, love abide, these three; but the greatest of these is love.

The Old Testament Song of Songs (known as the Song of Solomon in some translations) is a series of love poems or nuptial dialogue which is for the most part in the form of songs addressed by a man to a woman and by a woman to a man. The following is adapted from the Sixth Song:

Set me as a seal upon your arm
As a seal upon your heart
For love is as strong as death
Many waters cannot quench it
No flood can sweep it away.

Another appropriate passage is from Ruth:1:16, 17:

Entreat me not to leave you or to return from following you: for where you go I will go, and where you lodge I will lodge; your people shall be my people and your God my God; where you die I will die, and there will I be buried. May the Lord do so to me and more also if even death parts me from you.

Civil Ceremony

In Britain almost all weddings must be conducted in a place of worship or a building registered with the Superintendent Registrar of Marriage. In Australia, Canada and the United States, however, it is possible to get married virtually anywhere by a civil celebrant.

A civil celebration is far more flexible than a religious ceremony and can be adapted to any words and music chosen by the couple with the help of the celebrant. An increasing number of couples write their own words of commitment to each other. A typical civil ceremony will include a

welcoming address and statement by the celebrant, an exchange of vows by the couple, a declaration that the marriage has taken place, and the signing of the marriage certificate by the couple, the celebrant and two witnesses. The ceremony may incorporate prayers, readings, songs, poetry, the giving away of the bride and the exchange of rings. There may be elements of the traditional ceremony retained, or the ceremony may be entirely rewritten by the couple and the celebrant. The celebrant may put the traditional form of the question to the couple where the groom and bride are asked in turn,

... will you take ... to be your lawful wedded wife (husband)? Will you love, honor and keep her, in sickness and in health, for better for worse, richer or poorer, so long as you both shall live?

and each replies in turn, 'I will.' Or, the question could be varied as follows:

... will you take ... to be your lawful wedded wife (husband)? Will you love and respect her, be honest with her, and stand by her through whatever may come so you can genuinely share your life together?

Then the vows follow. The bride and groom face the celebrant, holding hands, and repeat the vows after the celebrant, the groom speaking first and then the bride. The vows may also be worded to suit the individual couple. They might say, for example,

I give myself to you, ... I will share my life with you, respect you, care for you, cherish and encourage you for all the days of our lives.

Or:

I ..., take you, ..., as my wife (husband). I pledge to share my life openly with you, to speak the truth to you, in love. I promise to honor and tenderly care for you, to cherish and encourage your own fulfillment as an individual for the rest of my life.

Or they may simply say,

I, ... call upon the persons here present to witness that I take you, ..., to be my lawful wife (husband).

After both have repeated their vows, the groom places the ring on the third finger of the bride's left hand, or the couple exchange rings, saying as they do so, if they wish,

With this ring I thee wed, with my body I thee honor and all my worldly goods with thee I share.

An alternative could be,

With this ring I wed you and pledge my faithful love.

The celebrant will then conclude the official ceremony by pronouncing the couple husband and wife.

Readings

To add personal warmth to a civil ceremony, a couple may wish to include a reading or special poem. This may be read by the celebrant, a special friend or by the bride or groom. A reading can be added at any time during the ceremony, but the title and author of the poem should be announced first. Some examples of readings are:

The Prophet

Love one another,
But make not a bond of love.
Let it rather be a moving sea
Between the shores of your souls
Fill each other's cup
But drink not from the same cup
Sing and dance together and be joyous,
But let each one of you be alone
Though they quiver with the same music
Give your hearts,
But not into each other's keeping
For only the hand of life
Can contain your hearts
And stand together
Yet not too near together
For the pillars of the temple stand apart
And the oak tree and the cypress
Grow not in each other's shadow.

— Kahlil Gibran

Love

Love is a very simple thing,
Love is a contented mind.
Love is tolerance, being warm,
Love is just being kind
Love is trusting, being sure,
As sure as there's starshine above,
That when the moment is at hand
You'll know this real meaning of love.

—Anonymous

My Love

My love surrounds the house in which you
dwell,
The place you work, the streets your feet have
known,
With more of tenderness than I can tell
And prayers that I have said for you alone.
If you are lonely, know that I am near:
If you are sad, my faith will comfort you.
The things you value I shall hold most dear,
Your happiness will make me happy too.
And be sure of this: Though you may travel far,
My love will guard you anywhere you are.

May love be with you through the flight of
years,
Then after storms, there always will be calm.
Though you have cause for heartache and for
tears,
Despair last not, where love is there for balm.

This be the prayer we breathe for you today:
When you have reached the summit of Life's
hill,
May it be possible for you to say,
'Married long years, but we are lovers still.'

— Anonymous

— Anonymous

We Will Not Wish You Joy

We will not wish you joy on this great day,
For joy is in your hearts and goes with you
Along the fragrant, mystic, sunlit way:
We will not wish you joy whilst love is new.

But this is our wish — May you be strong
enough
To shelter love, and keep it safe from harm,
When winds blow high, and roads are steep
and rough,
May you protect your love, preserve its charm.

When days are dark, may love be your sure
light.
When days are cold, may love be your bright
fire,
Your guiding star when Hope is out of sight,
The essence and the sun of your desire.

Love's Philosophy

The fountains mingle with the river,
And the rivers with the ocean,
The winds of heaven mix for ever
With a sweet emotion;
Nothing in the world is single;
All things by a law divine
In one another's being mingle
Why not I with thine?

See the mountains kiss high heaven,
And the waves clasp one another;
No sister flower would be forgiven
If it disdained its brother;
And the sunlight clasps the earth,
And the moonbeams kiss the sea,
What are all these kissings worth,
If thou kiss not me?

— Percy Bysshe Shelley

Choosing Music For the Ceremony

Your own personal selection of music allows you the artistic freedom to create an event full of joyful celebration and wonderful memories. A well-chosen selection will enhance and enrich your wedding service.

For a religious service you will be able to choose from an inspiring repertory of hymns, anthems, marches, processionals, organ music, choral music and solo singing. You will need to discuss with your clergyman what is considered suitable music. The organist will be able to advise on his or her repertoire and the capabilities of the organ. The organist and the church caretaker should also be consulted about the pealing of church bells. If you are having a choir sing at your wedding, choose their music with the help of the choirmaster.

You might like to include printed hymn and order-of-service sheets, which the ushers will hand out as the congregation enters.

Before the Ceremony

A very calming and mood-enhancing idea is to have a musical prelude as guests enter the church and take their places before the service begins. This could be in the form of an organ recital, a solo flute or a small chamber orchestra. Music played for about fifteen minutes before your arrival will provide special pleasure for guests and

will lead smoothly into the processional. It will also help prevent guests from noticing if you are a little late. The selections should be joyous and might include Bach's 'Sheep May Safely Graze,' 'Jesu, Joy of Man's Desiring,' 'Adagio in A Minor,' Beethoven's 'Joyful, Joyful, We Adore Thee,' Dvorak's 'Biblical Songs,' Handel's 'Water Music,' Liszt's 'Liebestraum.'

The Processional

It is important to have a practice session to check the length of the processional music piece against the time it takes to walk down the aisle. The classic bridal chorus from Wagner's *Lohengrin*, is familiar to us all as 'Here Comes the Bride.' However, you may think it is a little too common and prefer to have your own special favorite played instead. Other choices for the bride's processional might include Bach's 'Sinfonia from Wedding Cantata,' 'Fantasia in G,' Handel's 'Sarabande Suite 11,' 'The Arrival of the Queen of Sheba,' Mozart's 'Marriage of Figaro,' Pachelbel's 'Canon in D Minor,' Purcell's 'Trumpet, Tune and Air,' Stanley's 'Trumpet Tune.'

Hymns

Hymns will be part of the service, and since the guests are expected to join in it's best to choose those that people know and enjoy singing. You will not need more than three hymns. Some hymns are more appropriate than others for a wedding and you should read all the verses of the hymns you are considering. Well-known hymns suitable for a wedding include: 'Amazing Grace,' 'Come Down, O Love Divine,' 'Dear Lord and Father of Mankind,' 'Jerusalem,' 'Joyful, Joyful, We Adore Thee,' 'Love Divine All Love Excelling,' 'O, Perfect Love, All Human Thought Transcending,' 'Praise My Soul the King of Heaven,' 'The King of Love My Shepherd Is.'

Signing of the Registry

At the end of the ceremony the bridal party proceeds to the vestry for the signing of the registry. While they are doing this, it is customary for a favorite song or a piece of joyful music to be played for the waiting congregation. You might prefer an organ recital, or singing by a soloist or a full choir. Popular choices are Bach's 'Jesu, Joy of Man's Desiring,' 'Magnificat,' Beethoven's 'Joyful, Joyful, We Adore Thee,' Mozart's 'Laudate Dominum,' Purcell's 'Rejoice in the Lord Always,' Schubert's 'Ave Maria,' or Wood's 'O Thou the Central Orb.'

When the signing is complete, the wedding group emerges to the strains of the recessional, which is usually the wedding march from Mendelssohn's *A Midsummer Night's Dream*. Some alternatives to consider are Bach's 'Fantasia,' Clarke's 'Trumpet Voluntary,' Handel's 'Water Music,' 'Royal Fireworks Music,' Verdi's 'Grand March from *Aida*,' Vivaldi's 'The Four Seasons (Spring Movement),' or Widor's 'Toccata in F,' from Symphony No. 5.

Transport to the Ceremony

Many brides prefer the traditional mode of getting to the ceremony — by car. Others may prefer an elaborate carriage or even a fire engine.

Transportation can serve as the centerpiece of a theme wedding and can set the right mood for the day. For an old world look there are storybook carriages, complete with footmen in top hats and tails, pulled by beautifully groomed horses. The elegance of a twenties wedding can be enhanced by the bride arriving in a vintage Rolls Royce. For an informal, country-type wedding a bride may want a hayride with footmen dressed in checked shirts, jeans and hats.

There are ferries, speed boats and seaplanes for a wedding near the water. An automobile agency that caters to the film and television industry is the best approach if you want to hire the unusual such as a London cab, a hot rod, a fire engine, a period car or a motorcycle escort.

The classic look never dates, and when booking a luxury chauffeur-driven limousine you will have a very large choice of cars, for example Cadillac, Mercedes, Rolls Royce, Bentley, Ferrari and Jaguar in a range of such classic colors as white, silver, ivory and blue. It is important that you choose cars to suit the style of your wedding.

To find out what's available, inspect the vehicles the rental companies have on display. To ensure you get exactly what you want, bookings should be made as soon as you have worked out dates, times and locations. You will need to discuss fees, overtime charges, tips, the attire of the drivers, timing and parking.

How many cars you need depends on the number of people in your bridal party. Traditionally the bride travels to the ceremony in a car with her father, while her attendants ride in one or more additional automobiles. If the mode of transport is a horse-drawn carriage quite often only the bride will travel in the carriage. After the ceremony the bride and groom usually go to the reception in the vehicle she arrived in. Parents and attendants use other cars. Most rental cars take four people, but there are some that can take six.

If you do choose the romance and leisurely pace of a horse-drawn carriage, there are many styles to choose from: as well as landaus and broughams there are surreys, victorias, and hansom cabs. It is necessary to visit a horse and carriage service to see what the different carriages look like. Most carriage companies will include the footmen and drivers dressed in top hats and tails or in a vest which matches the color of the carriage in the cost of the hire. If you want the footmen and drivers to wear something different, there may be an extra charge.

Check with the carriage company as to what special insurance coverage it has and if the carriages have any modern

safety features to help them cope in ordinary traffic. You may have to alert local police or obtain a permit if you are using carriages or special transportation that can block or slow traffic.

After the bride and groom have left the site of the ceremony for the reception, it is the responsibility of the best man to make sure that all the guests have transport to the reception. Not all people have cars and it might be more efficient to hire a mini van for guests who don't drive.

≈ THE RECEPTION ≈

*W*eddings are wonderful affairs and should be fun, filled with special
moments of joy and celebration.

Celebration Ideas

Whether the gathering is large or
small, simple or elaborate the
following ideas may help you decide
on what type of reception is right
for you.

Tents or Canopies

If you are planning a home wedding
with a large number of guests,
consider hiring a tent. Rental firms
have tents in all sizes and colors that
can be erected in the garden around
virtually any garden feature: around
trees, on top of pools and over ponds.
You should be given a choice of
decorative lining, flooring and
heating. The decorative lining—
whether it be in pastel silk or in bright
stripes — can be chosen to match your
wedding theme. Rental firms are often
booked well in advance, so order as
soon as a date is decided.

Decorating a tent can be lots of fun,
but it can be very time-consuming.
You will need extra helping hands,
especially if you want to cover every
support pole with ivy or ribbon or turn
the tent into a fantasy setting. Here
are some ideas for decoration:
Ropings of leaves, blossoms and even
fruit-laden branches from citrus trees
attached to the poles are inexpensive,
fragrant, and will create a romantic
atmosphere.

Make roses a focal point. Have
generous centerpieces of full-blown
roses on every table. Rose floral chintz
tablecloths will enliven the neutral
space of a tent. Or attach masses of
single rosebuds to the sides of white
tablecloths, with the most attractive
buds across the front drop of the bridal
table.

When rental expenses are mounting
uncontrollably, borrow the table
settings. Borrowed tableware does not
have to be identical or matching, each
table can be set with an individual
look and in so doing you can create a
rich, picturesque presentation. Flower
arrangements can be made to colour
coordinate with each setting.

Conservatory

Surround yourself with plants and flowers by holding your reception in a conservatory or greenhouse. For a small wedding a domestic conservatory will provide romance and visual interest. For a large number of guests inquire at historic houses, botanic and zoological gardens, and other institutions. You might find an architectural gem.

All-Night Party

If your guests are young, or think they are young, hold an all-night party with dancing and finger food. Serve an extravagant midnight feast and breakfast before dawn.

A green-and-white color theme is a quick and easy way to create a striking setting. Drape each table with a white cloth, and pin or stitch long stems of trailing ivy in garlands around the edge of the cloth. Use forest green table napkins. Drape the poles of the tent with ivy and big white bows. Move in as many potted palms as you can borrow or hire. Use lots of foliage in giant floral decorations and use a few bold white flowers such as chrysanthemums, white hydrangeas and roses for impact. Hang green and white balloons and paper lanterns.

Medieval Feast

Turn an outdoor barbecue into a medieval fête. Provide a sit-down meal in a barn set with long trestle tables for the guests, and a large round table — as in King Arthur's day — for the bridal table. Decorate the tables with rich velvet swags and herb garlands and wreaths. Serve hearty food on large platters, and hire troubadours and musicians to play chamber music.

Old World Wedding

Arrive at the reception in a horse-drawn carriage. Use family heirlooms for an old world wedding— antique lace cloths on the tables, gleaming silver candelabra and cutlery and sparkling crystal glasses. Hire a palm court salon orchestra, a string ensemble, or an Andalusian guitarist to play poignant love ballads.

Garden Party

Plan ahead for a summer garden party when the garden is in full bloom with wall-to-wall flowers and the weather is pleasant. If you know well in advance when the wedding is to take place, then the garden, pots and hanging baskets can be specially planted with your color theme. Move containers of flowering plants to strategic positions, use flowery chintz tablecloths, have bowls of full-blown garden roses on the tables and decorate buckets of ice with fresh daisies. Cold buffet food can be served under a canopy to protect it from the sun.

Moonlit Cruise

For glamor and romance hire a luxury cruiser or sailing ship and celebrate on a moonlit cruise. Many companies cater for small or large weddings, from buffets to banquets. Some cruisers will have plenty of room for dancing.

Autumn Picnic

Autumn brings its own romance to lovers everywhere. Celebrate your wedding with an autumn picnic in a nearby park or woods. Have an extravagant menu, the best linen napkins, crystal goblets, and silver and china to enable you to witness the drama of autumn's display in style and comfort. Gypsy music would be wonderful in this setting.

Cocktail Party

A cocktail party is an elegant and easy way to entertain a large number of guests for a fairly short time. It encourages mingling and conversation, and it does not need to be restricted to the conventional cocktail hour of late afternoon or early evening. A cocktail party is perfect for a mid-morning

reception or in fact can be held at any hour up to around 7:00 PM. Hire waiters in black tie to bear trays of drinks the moment guests arrive and to pass the food. Plan for an exquisite presentation of uncluttered food. The music should be soft, cool, sophisticated jazz.

Taya and Blake
request the pleasure
of your company
to celebrate
their wedding
on February 2, 1991
at St Stephens Uniting Church
Chatswood
to be followed by
a reception at
North Curl Curl
Surf Life Saving Club
Curl Curl

R S V P
December 31, 1991
3/10 Wheeler Pde Dee Why : 982 3549

Ethnic Celebration

An ethnic background could set the tone for food, drink, decor and music. The inclusion of national dishes pays tribute to family backgrounds and adds personal flair. Authentic national dress might also be considered for the ceremony. A Greek wedding party could begin with ouzo and could have joyful bouzouki music playing in the background. A Scottish wedding could have all the trappings of bagpipes, hearty Scottish food, tartan tablecloths and wall hangings, cheerful open fires, Scotch whisky, kilts and highland dancing. Flamenco music as an accompaniment to tapas, gazpacho, paella, wonderful sherries and sangria is certain to give life to a Spanish wedding.

Afternoon Tea Party

Turn an afternoon tea party into one of celebration and fantasy with a string quartet or a high energy jazz group dressed in gangster gear. Use pretty, fine bone china, crystal sherry glasses and elegant champagne flutes and cloths of delicate lace and serve a sumptuous afternoon feast. Sherry, Madeira and champagne all complement afternoon tea parties whether the food is savoury or sweet.

Hotel Reception

For a very large gathering— and for a minimum of worries — consider holding your reception at an hotel. You will be assured of professional service, built-in decor (often very elaborate in old hotels), a variety of menu choices, and experienced staff to guide you to the best decisions. Some hotels provide an in-house florist, a dance floor and music and a bridal suite for the wedding night. When you have found the hotel of your choice it is vital to book everything well in advance. Go over every step with the catering manager and have everything spelled out in a contract. Most hotels ask for an advance deposit.

Further Suggestions

Small table lamps can provide romantic lighting if you are holding your reception in a tent or hall.

An evening barbecue can be lit with special outdoor candles.

Decorate the center of long tables with a row of orchids and ivy interspersed with candles.

Simple lights behind large flower arrangements add sparkle and glamor to the flowers and fill the room with life.

Provide good lighting for catering staff to work by.

Ensure driveways, swimming pools and garden paths are adequately lit.

Personal Touches at Home

These days a wedding can be very expensive. By having an at-home reception you can save on the rental fee of a reception site as well as have the personal surroundings that no other setting can provide.

Whether or not you use a caterer will depend on you, your budget and the size of the gathering. Once the number of guests goes beyond twenty or twenty-five, it is unlikely you will have sufficient table and glassware or sufficient staff for the reception and you will need to consider supplementary equipment and professional help. A caterer will usually supply all the tableware.

There are many ways to transform your home into a place of comfort and celebration. The success of a reception party at home depends on the planning you put into it beforehand, details are important. Many people are prepared to help out at a wedding, so accept any help offered. Do as much preparation as possible before the day, such as laying the tables, setting up drink stations and arranging flowers. It is important not to be exhausted on the day of the wedding as you will want to make everyone welcome and relaxed. The following are ideas that can be carried out in advance of the big day.

A handmade banner welcoming the newlyweds can be hung between two trees or across the front verandah.

Decorate the bathrooms with flowers, potpourri, fresh soap, hand towels and cologne. Ensure a plentiful supply of toilet paper.

Arrange where coats, wraps and bags are to go. If it is to be a bedroom, dress old teddy bears and stuffed toys with large bowties.

Dress the pool with floating camellias or magnolia blossoms.

Make sure there are adequate parking facilities or give clear instructions to guests on alternatives for parking.

If you are having a buffet table, serve food from the table set in the middle of the room. Remember, you will need one buffet table per seventy guests.

Have a bar or waiter just inside the house to provide drinks for guests held up at the receiving line.

Plan for a suitable area for the formal photographs to be taken without encroaching too much on the rest of the party.

Have wood ready for fireplaces. A blazing fire creates a welcoming atmosphere in the winter months.

Have a guest book ready at the entrance for each guest to sign as they enter the reception. These albums can be obtained from stationery shops and department stores.

You will need lots and lots of ice. If you have to place it in plain containers, decorate them with fresh daisies or ferns.

Make sure you provide ashtrays. Place troughs with sand in areas such as patios, porches and hallways where there is no place to put ashtrays.

Beautiful flowers in the home will immediately evoke a mood of celebration. Place a large arrangement at the entrance to the house, at the place where photographs are to be

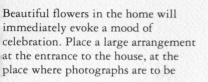

Music at the Reception

Whether your reception is a light wedding breakfast or a full-scale dinner dance, music will add greatly to the atmosphere and festivities.

There are endless choices from the wonderful world of music, but whether you hire a solo violinist, a swing band or a disc jockey, you will need a clear idea of the music you want and how to make the necessary arrangements.

taken, on the buffet table, on mantelpieces, where the speeches are to be given or any other places where they will be noticed. If you do not have a lot of flowers, then use plenty of foliage. Position arrangements where they won't get knocked over and make sure to leave room for guests to circulate.

Selecting the Music

At a small wedding you might have a pianist, a guitarist, a quartet or any group that plays dinner music. At a large wedding where there will be dancing you may prefer a swing band, a Latin American group or a disco. For an outdoor reception a string ensemble would be ideal, and strings plus flute or classical guitar would be perfect for a romantic wedding in any setting. A Dixieland band would be wonderful for a reception on a boat, while a sophisticated jazz group would be a good choice if you are holding the reception in an hotel or restaurant.

There are a lot of mixed marriages today and lively ethnic music and traditional dances are a wonderful way for both sides of the family to mix together. National dances are usually easy to learn and are a sure way to get everyone up and dancing and are especially popular with older family members. There is the Spanish flamenco; the Greek chain dance *kalamatianos*; the Irish jig; the Italian *tarantella*; the Polish dollar dance, where guests pay a dollar to dance with the bride or groom; and the Israeli *hora,* usually danced to *Hava Nagila*.

It is likely you will have representatives from several generations at your wedding — from small children to grandparents — so it is a good idea to select songs that will appeal to a wide range of ages and musical tastes. Remember not to seat grandparents or other elderly guests too close to the source of the music, and for dancing, softer tunes should be interspersed with louder current favorites — a steady flow of very loud modern music could be unpleasant for older guests.

Different music will be appropriate at different stages of the proceedings. You will need light and romantic background music during the introductions. Light jazz, instrumentals or show music could be played during the meal.

The Bridal Waltz

Dancing music may be played before the meal and continued between courses, or it may begin after the meal. If dancing is the order of the day, it is customary for the newly married couple to take to the floor for the first dance. Some couples choose to start the bridal dance at the beginning of the reception in order to get the party going. Some favorite first-dance songs are 'As Time Goes By,' 'You Are the Sunshine of My Life,' 'Endless Love,' 'The Greatest Love of All,' 'Saving All My Love for You,' 'I'll Be With You in Apple Blossom Time,' 'Hello Young Lovers,' 'Thank Heaven for Little Girls,' 'Moon River,' 'Lara's Theme,' 'Always,' 'Embraceable You.'

Hiring Musicians

A good working relationship with a professional musician or disc jockey is critical to the success of your wedding music. You will need to check their repertoires and styles. A good band or disc jockey will play different music for different groups of people and you should be able to influence the style of music that will be played during various parts of the proceedings. Go over song choices with the musicians or disc jockey well before the wedding, but do allow some flexibility with the order of songs.

Musical Checklist

Choose a band only after you have heard them play.

Explain your wishes carefully.

Get written confirmation of the booking and fee.

Find out overtime rates.

Specify how you wish the group or disc jockey to dress.

Establish how often the band will take a break and for how long.

Determine whether the band will play tapes on a sound system during breaks.

Ensure that there is ample space to set up equipment and that there are plenty of electrical outlets.

Remember to specify which tune you want for the bridal waltz.

Grace

Grace is often omitted nowadays, but for a sit-down meal some couples think it is a good time to take a quiet moment to thank God, and for all to start the celebratory meal together. Grace should be said by a minister, if present. However, the duty can be undertaken by the bride's father. It is best to keep grace short and simple. One of the following forms of grace would be appropriate:

For what we are about to receive, may the Lord make us truly thankful.

For our families, our friends and for this food which you give us, we thank you, Lord.

We thank you, our Father, for good food, which brings health and human love, which brings happiness.

Receive our thanks, O Lord, for this food and for this happy day.

Everyone says, 'Amen.'

Toasts and Speeches

Many people feel the wedding celebration would not be complete without a few words from someone from the bridal party. Toasts and speeches are not really obligatory and some couples do without them altogether, particularly at a reception following a civil ceremony or a second marriage. Others believe that a toast to the bride and groom and the groom's response are essential.

Traditionally the speakers are men, although these days it is not uncommon for the bride and the bride's mother to be requested to say a few words also.

A number of toasts and speeches are possible. Someone closely associated with the couple who is an experienced speaker may be invited to say a few words, or a family friend may toast the couple's parents. When there is a toast to the parents, usually the male parent responds.

At an informal reception where there are to be no speeches, the best man could ask for silence and offer his toast to the bride and groom as soon as all the guests have arrived and been served drinks. At many weddings nowadays a single toast, given by the best man, has replaced the tradition of numerous speeches.

Most of us are newcomers to public speaking, so here are some points to keep in mind. The speeches need not be too serious or sentimental. They should be sincere and happy, and for those given by the best man a bit of humor is in order. They should be appropriate and to the point and no more than two to five minutes long. It is a good idea to write the speech in full and to learn it by heart. Write your speech on index cards and highlight the key points and names of people you want to mention. Keep the cards with you as a reminder should you forget your words. This will enable you to keep your head up and look at your audience as you speak.

The following is a traditional sequence of toasts and speeches. Even at a formal wedding, however, the sequence does not have to be strictly followed, it's entirely up to you.

The father of the bride or a close friend or relative proposes the health, happiness and prosperity of the newlyweds. He may wish to mention the pleasure he and his wife have experienced in raising their daughter, a significant or amusing episode in her life, a welcome into the family of the new son-in-law, a welcome and thanks to the groom's parents, and a tribute to the bride's mother for all her efforts in arranging the wedding. He may also wish to thank everyone for coming to celebrate his daughter's wedding. The newlyweds remain seated and do not drink the toast.

The bridegroom replies and thanks everyone on behalf of his wife and himself. He thanks the bride's parents for the reception and anything they may have provided for the couple's future, the guests for coming and for their good wishes and gifts, the clergyman for his service, his parents for their kindness and help, the best man for his assistance and the attendants for their help. He closes his speech by proposing a toast to the bridesmaids.

The best man then replies on behalf of the bridesmaids. His speech should be light and as far as possible filled with humor. He will shower praise on the bride and refer to the goom's luck on winning the bride. He might flatter the bridesmaids or refer to the end of the groom's bachelor outings. He will then read the messages of congratulations and good wishes that have arrived for the newlyweds. This can provide an opportunity for some jokes and frivolity, although he should omit any messages that may be offensive. If there are a great number of messages it is not a good idea to read all of them — this can take hours and can become boring. When he has finished his speech, he may wish to lead the bridal table in a toast to the guests.

Getaways

If the bride and groom have used a hired vehicle to get to the ceremony and wish to leave the reception in their own transport, it is up to the best man to get their car to the reception. He should also put the couple's luggage in the car and drive them to the airport or railway station if necessary.

Some couples might wish to make a grand exit in a hot-air balloon, a helicopter or chartered airplane. Whatever the form of transport, attendants must be very careful when applying 'Just Married' decorations. They must never damage paint work, use decorations that will block the driver's vision or make loud noises that will interfere with hearing. Trailing ribbons, a 'Just Married' heart and flowers are fine. Old shoes and tins should be tied well out of harm's way.

≈ WAYS TO SAY THANK YOU ≈

Often presents begin to arrive as soon as the invitations have been received. Ideally the bride should send a thank-you letter as soon as she receives each present up to the day of the wedding.

This will help her find spontaneous wording and avoid an enormous task when she returns from the honeymoon. All presents should be acknowledged within a month after the honeymoon.

From the moment you draw up the guest list it is a good idea to keep a systematic record, file or computer list of addresses of the guests, when the gifts were received, a description of each gift and the date of posting of the thank-you note. This record will also be useful for future celebrations such as christenings and anniversaries.

Traditionally the bride writes the thank-you notes, but will often enlist the help of the groom, especially if a present is from a member of his family.

Stationery

Thank-you notes should always be handwritten on good quality notepaper. Printed thank-you notes with fill-in spaces are not acceptable for weddings. Most people give a lot of thought to a wedding present and an expression of appreciation should be thoughtful and sincere.

If you are ordering personalized stationery, it is a good idea to have your new address printed in the top right-hand corner. This saves you having to write the address out each time and advises everyone of your new address. This is less expensive than having cards printed with the bride's maiden name and address for use before the ceremony and another set for use after the ceremony.

A creative bride may wish to press flowers from her bouquet and make her own personalized cards. Good quality blank cards for this purpose can be bought from stationery shops and art supply stores.

You may wish to place a photograph of the wedding on the front of the thank-you notes. These can be ordered from your photographer, but will not be ready to be sent until you return from your honeymoon.

Wording

Thank-you notes should always be worded from both partners. However only the writer should sign the note. The bride should use her maiden name for all letters written before the wedding.

Each note should include a reference to the present itself and how you plan to use it. Try to include at least one other personal message.

The wording may be formal or informal depending on your relationship with the person who sent the gift. Above all, your sincerity must come through. The following examples may give you some ideas.

Dear Mr and Mrs Richards,

We are delighted with the wonderful juice extractor you so kindly gave us and which is in daily use.

Thank you very much for such a useful present and for taking part in our wedding day. We both hope to see you again soon.

Dear Jane and Peter,

We have already found the perfect photos for the stunning picture frames you sent us. They look great on the mantelpiece. Call in on Saturday.

Other Thank Yous

Other people who may need special thanks may be the volunteer flower committee at the place of worship or a friend who sang at the wedding. If the reception was at the family home, kind neighbors might need to be thanked for lending equipment, cooking or donating flowers from their gardens. Anyone who helped clean up (aside from the catering staff) will need the warmest thank you. All those who have sent messages of congratulations should also be thanked.

Mothers must not be forgotten and some couples give their mothers each a lovely surprise bouquet as they leave for their honeymoon.

Presents to attendants are usually given at the rehearsal dinner the night before the wedding, or on the wedding day. However, you may wish to buy them a special exotic thank-you gift while you are on your honeymoon. Do not forget the pages and flower girls.

≈ WEDDING TRADITIONS ≈ AND SUPERSTITIONS

The wedding ring has long been a physical symbol of the covenant between the two people who are being joined in marriage.

The Wedding Ring

The moment the wedding ring is placed on the finger is often the most significant part of the ceremony.

The ring is usually an unadorned, simple gold wedding band. The plain uninterrupted circle is an emblem of perfect union. Gold is chosen not because it is a precious metal but because it symbolizes purity of intent.

Tradition has it that it is placed on the third finger of the bride's left hand because it was once believed that a vein called the *Vena amoris* ran straight from this finger to the heart.

It is considered very bad luck to drop the wedding ring on the wedding day.

Wedding Attire

*Something old,
Something new,
Something borrowed,
Something blue,
And a silver sixpence in her shoe.*

This saying dates back to Victorian times and whether brides really believe in it or not, many try to arrange their wedding attire accordingly even if only for fun.

Something old represents links with the bride's family and the past and many brides choose to wear a piece of antique family jewelry or use an antique cake knife at the reception.

Something new represents success and good fortune in the bride's new life. The wedding dress is most often chosen as the new item.

Something borrowed reminds the bride that friends may always be helpful when needed. The borrowed object may be anything from a veil to

Married in white, you have chosen aright.
Married in blue, your lover is true.
Married in pink, your fortunes will sink.
Married in green, you will not long be seen.
Married in red, you'll wish you were dead.
Married in yellow, ashamed of the fellow.
Married in brown, you'll live out of town.
Married in gray, you'll live far away.
Married in black, you'll wish you were
back.

a lace handkerchief, but whatever it is it must be returned to the owner to fulfill the superstition.

Something blue is the emblem of loyalty and faithfulness. Many brides wear a blue garter or a blue bow on the undergarments.

A silver sixpence in her shoe is to wish the bride future wealth.

There are many superstitions associated specifically with the wedding dress. It is supposed to be unlucky for the bride to try on the wedding dress and the veil in its entirety before the wedding day and the bridegroom must not see his bride in the dress before the wedding ceremony.

As to the color of the wedding gown, it appears that blue and white are the lucky colors:

The Bridal Bouquet

In olden times the bridal bouquet formed part of the wreaths and garlands worn by both the bride and groom. They were considered a symbol of happiness. In Wales bridesmaids are given myrtle sprigs from the bride's bouquet to plant. Tradition has it that if one takes root, the young woman will marry soon. Today the practice of tossing the bouquet is a refined development of throwing the garter. The lucky lady who catches the bouquet is believed to be the next to marry.

The Garter

The custom of throwing the garter began in France when pieces of bridal attire were considered lucky. The bride would throw the garter to the guests at the wedding feast and whoever caught it would supposedly be blessed with good luck. In the United States, the groom removes the bride's garter and throws it to the unmarried men. The man who catches it is thought to be the one who will marry next. He places the garter on the leg of the woman who catches the bridal bouquet.

Other Superstitions

Church Bells

The pealing of bells was supposed to
drive out evil spirits — what a joyful
way to drive away the demons and at
the same time let everyone know the
marriage has taken place.

Horseshoes

Horseshoes are an
ancient symbol of
fertility and good
luck. The
horseshoe must be
carried or stored
with the ends
pointing upwards
in order to keep
the luck in.

The Breaking of Glass

The breaking of glass by the groom is
a well-known element of Jewish
wedding ceremonies. It symbolizes the
destruction of the temple in Jerusalem
and serves as a reminder of the joy and
sorrow in the world. Today it is
considered to be a symbol of good luck
and signals the end of the marriage
ceremony.

Shoes

The tradition of tying shoes to the vehicle in which the bride and groom leave the reception goes back to Anglo-Saxon weddings when shoes were considered a symbol of authority. The father of the bride would give one of the bride's shoes to the new husband, who would then tap his wife on the head with the tip to signify that he would be the master throughout their marriage. In Greek ceremonies today, the dominating partner is decided by whoever — the bride or groom — is the first to tread on the other's foot at a designated stage of the ceremony.

Carrying the Bride over the Threshold

It was considered extremely bad luck for the bride to stumble on entering her house for the first time. This is one of the reasons why the bridegroom carries the bride over the threshold. Another old Roman explanation is that she was not to touch the house until she was officially part of it by partaking in the eating of the wedding cake at the hearth of the house.

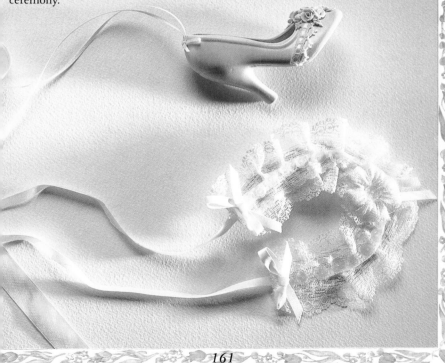

Rice or Confetti

The throwing of rice or confetti goes back to an ancient fertility rite that took place at weddings. The ancient Greeks poured flour and sweets over the bridal couple; the Italians small cakes; and the French wheat chaff.

These days rice, confetti or sugar-coated almonds are thrown at the couple for good luck. However, because of the litter this causes, it is becoming more common for the 'confetti-throwing' to take place as the couple leaves for their honeymoon rather than as they leave the church. Fresh or dried rose petals are increasingly used instead of rice or confetti — rose petals do not create litter and make a much more pleasant and fragrant send-off. Another lovely and fun way to send off the bride and groom is to give the guests bottles of children's bubbles to blow their good wishes to the couple.

Traditional Wedding Anniversaries

First
Cotton

Second
Paper

Third
Leather

Fourth
Silk

Fifth
Wood

Sixth
Iron

Seventh
Wool

Eighth
Bronze

Ninth
Pottery

Tenth
Tin

Twelfth
Linen

Fifteenth
Crystal

Twentieth
China

Twenty-fifth
Silver

Thirtieth
Pearls

Thirty-fifth
Coral

Fortieth
Ruby

Forty-fifth
Sapphire

Fiftieth
Gold

Fifty-fifth
Emerald

Sixtieth
Diamond

Seventy-fifth
Diamond

≈ ACKNOWLEDGMENTS ≈

The publishers would like to thank:

≈ ≈ ≈

Mary Turansky
The Queen Street Flower Shop, Sydney
for beautiful flowers

≈

Perry Snodgrass
Perry Snodgrass Catering, Sydney
and Sophie Lyn, Chef
Perry Snodgrass Catering, Sydney
for providing the menus and recipes
on pages 94-95, and pages 100-107
and all the food

≈

Shirley Jones
The Avenue Bridal Boutique, Sydney

≈

André Martin, photographer

≈

Karen Carter and Anna Soo, stylists

≈

Alma Williams

≈